2002

Revising Oral Theory

GARLAND STUDIES IN MEDIEVAL LITERATURE
VOLUME 16
GARLAND REFERENCE LIBRARY OF THE HUMANITIES
VOLUME 2104

Garland Studies in Medieval Literature

Paul E. Szarmach and Christopher Kleinhenz
General Editors

REVISING ORAL THEORY
FORMULAIC COMPOSITION
IN OLD ENGLISH AND
OLD ICELANDIC VERSE

PAUL ACKER

GARLAND PUBLISHING, INC.
A MEMBER OF THE TAYLOR & FRANCIS GROUP
NEW YORK AND LONDON
1998

Library of Congress Cataloging-in-Publication Data

Acker, Paul.
    Revising oral theory : formulaic composition in Old English and
Old Icelandic verse / Paul Acker.
        p.   cm. — (Garland studies in medieval literature ; v. 16)
        Includes bibliographical references and index.
        ISBN 0-8153-3102-9 (alk. paper)
        1. English poetry—Old English, ca. 450–1100—History and criticism.
2. Literature, Comparative—English (Old) and Old Norse.   3. Literature,
Comparative—Old Norse and English (Old)   4. Old Norse poetry—
History and criticism.   5. Oral-formulaic analysis.   6. Oral tradition—
England.   7. Oral tradition—Iceland. 8. Rhetoric, Medieval.   I. Title.
II. Series.
    PR179.07A25   1998
    829'.109—dc21   98-11371

Printed on acid-free, 250-year-life paper
Manufactured in the United States of America

SERIES PREFACE

Garland Studies in Medieval Literature (GSML) is a series of interpretative and analytic studies of the Western European literatures of the Middle Ages. It includes both outstanding recent dissertations and book-length studies, giving junior scholars and their senior colleagues the opportunity to publish their research.

In accordance with GSML policy the general editors have sought to welcome submissions representing any of the various schools of criticism and interpretation. Western medieval literature, with its broad historical span, multiplicity and complexity of language and literary tradition, and special problems of textual transmission and preservation as well as varying historical contexts, is both forbidding and inviting to scholars. It continues to offer rich materials for virtually every kind of literary approach that maintains a historical dimension. In establishing a series in an eclectic literature, the editors acknowledge and respect the variety of texts and textual possibilities and the "resisting reality" that confronts medievalists in several forms: on parchment, in mortar, or through icon. It is no mere imitative fallacy to be eclectic, empirical, and pragmatic in the face of this varied literary tradition that has so far defied easy formulation. The cultural landscape of the twentieth century is littered with the debris of broken monomyths predicated on the Middle Ages, the autocratic Church and the Dark Ages, for example, or conversely, the romanticized versions of love and chivalry.

The openness of the series means in turn that scholars, and particularly beginning scholars, need not pass an a priori test of "correctness" in their ideology, method, or critical position. The studies published in GSML must be true to their premises, complete within their articulated limits, and accessible to a multiple readership. Each study will advance the knowledge of the literature under discussion, opening it up for further consideration and creating intellectual value. It is also hoped that each volume, while bridging the gap between contemporary perspective and past reality, will make old texts new again. In this way the literature will remain primary, the method secondary.

Christopher Kleinhenz
University of Wisconsin-Madison

Paul E. Szarmach
Western Michigan University

Contents

Preface

The following monograph is a revised and updated version of the dissertation I submitted for a Ph.D. in English from Brown University. This dissertation developed as a result of three experiences beyond my introductory coursework: an advanced tutorial in Old English, a Fulbright year in Iceland, and a year teaching Old Icelandic at Brown. For the first of these, I would like to thank Professor Geoffrey Russom, who not only first introduced me to Old English, directed my dissertation, and generously responded to many of my interim projects, but also in his own work has provided a model of judicious and sensitive analysis.

I thank the Fulbright Institute for sending me to Iceland, where I researched my fourth chapter and received bibliographical assistance from Bjarni Guðnason and Vésteinn Ólason, who were then at Háskóli Íslands. Jón Friþjónsson, also of Háskóli Íslands, instructed me in Modern Icelandic. The increased facility I gained as a result has made my reading of Old Icelandic texts all the more pleasurable.

During my last year at Brown, Professor Russom and Professor William Crossgrove helped secure for me an opportunity to teach Old Icelandic. Out of this experience grew the discussion of themes in my third chapter. Also during this year, Professor Donald K. Fry, then of SUNY Stony Brook, and Professor S.F.D. Hughes of Purdue University agreed to act as my second and third readers. Their collective generosity meant that my dissertation benefited from three sets of informed commentary. When I attended a seminar on "*Beowulf* and Germanic Antiquity" organized by Joseph Harris and Thomas Hill and funded by the National Endowment for the Humanities, Professor Hill was kind enough to read through and comment on a revised version of my dissertation.

I thank the editors of *Language and Style* for publishing a version of my second chapter. Versions of my second and third chapters were delivered at the Patristic Medieval and Renaissance Studies Conference (Villanova) and the International Congress on Medieval Studies at Western Michigan University (Kalamazoo). My thanks are due to Professor Phillip Pulsiano and Professor Hughes for organizing the conference sections.

My computer files were reformatted expertly and speedily by my student, Deborah Hyland. My colleagues Clarence Miller, Vincent Casaregola, and Anthony Hasler were gracious enough to read through the manuscript and make useful suggestions.

For encouraging me to develop this monograph, I thank Gary Kuris of Garland Publishing and Paul E. Szarmach, co-editor of Garland Studies in Medieval Literature, and I thank Leo Balk for honoring Gary's intentions after his departure.

Texts and Abbreviations

Text references are to the ASPR (ed. Krapp & Dobbie—see Bibliography) for all Old English poems except *Beowulf*, which I cite from Klaeber's edition (although I do not reproduce his italics for emendations, or macrons for vowel quantity). Citations from Eddic poems refer to Neckel & Kuhn (fourth edition); when quoting Dronke's edition I have supplied her stanza numbers where these differ. The text of the Old Icelandic and Old Norwegian rune poems is cited from Dickins, and a few other Old Icelandic poems are cited from Heusler & Ranisch, Gordon, or C. Tolkien as indicated. Old Icelandic names are given throughout in normalized Old Icelandic rather than anglicized or Modern Icelandic forms; hence Sigurðr rather than Sigurd or Sigurður. Following Icelandic practice, I employ "ǫ" for Old Icelandic 'hooked o' and "æ" for the 'oe' digraph; I also employ Kellogg's normalized Eddic titles (*Concordance*) rather than Neckel & Kuhn's diplomatic ones.

Title abbreviations for Old English poems are those recommended by Magoun ("Abbreviated Titles") and employed in Bessinger's concordance (where they are listed, xiii–xv); for Old Icelandic poems, those employed in Kellogg's concordance (which are modelled on Magoun's abbreviations and are more perspicuous than Neckel & Kuhn's). A few other title abbreviations (in Chapter One especially) derive from the scholar providing the citations.

And (OE): *Andreas*, ASPR 2
ASPR: *The Anglo-Saxon Poetic Records*, ed. Krapp & Dobbie
Atm (OI): *Atlamál*, Kuhn 248
Æl (OE): prose works of Ælfric, cited by Hoffmann
BlH (OE): prose *Blickling Homilies*, ed. Morris
Bwf (OE): *Beowulf*, ed. Klaeber

Chr (OE): *Christ*, ASPR 3

Dan (OE): *Daniel*, ASPR 1

Dipl. (OI): prose diplomata, cited by Cleasby & Vigfusson

DOE: *Dictionary of Old English*

Ebr (OI): *Eddubrot*, Kuhn 315

Ele (OE): *Elene*, ASPR 1

eME: early Middle English

Exo (OE): *Exodus*, ASPR 1

Ffn (OI): *Fáfnismál*, Kuhn 180

Fms (OI): prose *Fornmanna sögur*, cited by Cleasby & Vigfusson

Gðh (OI): *Guðrúnarhvöt*, Kuhn 264

Gðk I (OI): *Guðrúnarkviða in fyrsta*, Kuhn 202

Gðk III (OI): *Guðrúnarkviða in þriðja*, Kuhn 232

Gen (OE): *Genesis (A & B)*, ASPR 1

GfM (OE): *The Gifts of Men*, ASPR 3

Glc (OE): *Guthlac*, ASPR 3

Grm (OI): *Grímnismál*, Kuhn 57

Grp (OI): *Grípisspá*, Kuhn 164

H: Old Frisian laws, cited by Hoffmann

Háv (OI): *Hávamál*, Kuhn 17

HbM (OE): *The Husband's Message*, ASPR 3

Hel.: *Heliand* (Old Saxon), cited by Hoffmann

HHu I (OI): *Helgakviða Hundingsbana in fyrri*, Kuhn 130

HHu II (OI): *Helgakviða Hundingsbana önnur*, Kuhn 150

Hlð (OI): *Hlöðskviða*, ed. C. Tolkien sts. 74–107

Hmð (OI): *Hamðismál*, Kuhn 269

HrB (OI): *Helreið Brynhildar*, Kuhn 219

Jg2 (OE): *The Judgment Day II*, ASPR 6

Jln (OE): *Juliana*, ASPR 3

Lay (eME): Layamon's *Brut*, ed. Brook & Leslie

MB (OE): *The Meters of Boethius*, ASPR 5

MCh (OE): *The Metrical Charms*, ASPR 6

ME: Middle English

MED: *Middle English Dictionary*, ed. Kuhn

Mld (OE): *The Battle of Maldon*, ASPR 6

Mx1 (OE): *Maxims I*, ASPR 3

OE: Old English

OED2: *Oxford English Dictionary*, 2nd ed.

OI: Old Icelandic

OHG: Old High German (used for unspecified citations in Hoffmann)

OS: Old Saxon

P (OE): *The Metrical Psalms of the Paris Psalter*, ASPR 5

Phx (OE): *The Phoenix*, ASPR 3

Pra (OE): *A Prayer*, ASPR 6

R (OE): *Riddles*, ASPR 3

Rgn (OI): *Reginsmál*, Kuhn 173

Rsg (OE): *Resignation*, ASPR 3

Run (OE): *The Rune Poem*, ASPR 6

Sfr (OE): *The Seafarer*, ASPR 3

SFt (OE): *The Seasons for Fasting*, ASPR 6

Sgk I (OI): *Sigurðarkviða in meiri (Brot)*, Kuhn 198

Sgk II (OI): *Sigurðarkviða in skamma*, Kuhn 207

Vfþ (OI): *Vafþrúðnismál*, Kuhn 45

Wds (OE): *Widsith*, ASPR 3

WfL (OE): *The Wife's Lament*, ASPR 3

Whl (OE): *The Whale*, ASPR 3

Wulf. (OE): Wulfstan homilies (prose), ed. Bethurum

XSt (OE): *Christ and Satan*, ASPR 1

Introduction

In the nineteenth century a number of scholars focused their attention on the recurrent phrases found in Homeric and Old Germanic texts. Schmidt called these phrases *formulas*, and Sievers noted 'pan-Germanic' formulas in his edition of the Old Saxon *Heliand*. Milman Parry, however, is generally credited with providing the first cohesive explanation, *oral-formulaic theory*, to account for the presence of these formulas. In 1928 he argued that Homeric epithets, such as "swift-footed Achilles," were chosen according to metrical needs. After studying oral poets at work in Yugoslavia, he proposed that a knowledge of formulas was what enabled the oral epic poet to improvise on traditional themes. Parry's student Albert Lord presented this theory in its best known form in *The Singer of Tales*, which appeared in 1960.

In the meantime, however, Lord had introduced Magoun to the theory. In 1953, Magoun cited cross-references from the Anglo-Saxon corpus to illustrate that the beginning of *Beowulf* was "some seventy per cent" formulaic ("Oral Formulaic," 450). Magoun's students Creed ("Studies") and Diamond presented similar cases for all of *Beowulf* and the works of Cynewulf. Shortly thereafter Magoun, Crowne, Bonjour, Fry ("Hero," "Heroine," "Themes"), Greenfield and others began to isolate *themes*, the larger building-blocks of oral-formulaic composition.

In the succeeding decades a large body of corrective criticism has developed, addressing such issues as how to assess the oral versus literary qualities of the poems and how to define the formula in terms that best suit Anglo-Saxon poetic practice. One of the more persuasive early articles was by H.L. Rogers, who in 1966 showed how all parts of Parry's definition of the formula had been ignored in these Anglo-Saxon applications. Parry's definition was "a group of words which is regularly employed under the same metrical conditions to express a given essential idea" (see Lord, *Singer*, 30). In the work of Magoun and his students, this definition had been relaxed to include "groups" as small as gerundive inflections; "regularly employed," as verified by a "hard core of frequency," had lapsed into "generally useful." Larry Benson, also writing in 1966, argued that most of the extant Anglo-Saxon poems—many of which are close translations of Latin originals—could not have been orally improvised.[1] (The term oral-formulaic now often refers not to the oral composition of a given work, but rather to its employment of formulas that are the inheritance, most scholars would still argue, of an oral culture.)[2] Whallon demonstrated that Anglo-Saxon poetry differs greatly from Homeric in the matter of formulaic economy. Fry ("Formulas," "Themes," "Variation"), Cassidy, Curschmann and Quirk also proposed modifications in oral-formulaic theory as applied to Anglo-Saxon verse. In *The Lyre and the Harp* (1969), Ann Watts presented a book-length appraisal of these various modifications.

More recently Joseph Harris, in an article discussed in Chapter Four below ("Oral Poetry"), has provided a schema for classifying varieties of formulaic composition and transmission that represents a considerable advance upon the earlier oral/written dichotomy. In a widely known book-length study, Walter Ong has shown that throughout the Middle Ages aspects of literary and oral culture were complexly intertwined. Geoffrey Russom ("Artful Avoidance") has contributed to the discussion of formulaic economy by demonstrating how Anglo-Saxon poets, even when writing repetitive sequences, consistently "avoid the useful phrase." John Miles Foley ("Literary Art") has argued that shorter, Christian Serbo-Croatian poems overlooked by Parry provide closer analogues to Anglo-Saxon formulaic practice. Foley compiled critical surveys and an annotated bibliography of oral-formulaic studies through 1982,[3] and A. Olsen offered critical surveys for Old English in 1986 and 1988.

In three successive monographs (1988, 1990 and 1991), Foley explored oral aesthetics in Homeric, Serbo-Croatian and Old English poetry. His attention, in *Traditional Oral Epic* especially, to a wide spectrum of "traditional rules" for phraseology is much in sympathy with my approach via different levels of formulaic composition. Incorporating insights from speech-act and reception theory, Foley advocates a shift from a mechanistic oral-formulaic theory to a more comprehensive "oral theory." In 1990, Katherine O'Brien O'Keeffe published a monograph in the series Cambridge Studies in Anglo-Saxon England in which she traced "developing literacy" in the Old English manuscript record. In 1995, Francelia Clark offered a book-length study of the theme in Serbo-Croatian and Old English poetry. 1995 also saw the posthumous publication of Lord's magisterial look back on the reception of his work. He replied to many of the critical objections mentioned above and incorporated many of the revisions that scholars had made in adapting oral theory to Old English verse.

Lord's two monographs thus effectively bookend the transition of oral-formulaic theory to *oral theory*, as it is now often called,[4] a transition not unparalleled in the development of critical theory in literary studies. I am not aware of any previous attempt to situate oral-formulaic theory within a larger theoretical context, but surely a case could be made that oral-formulaic theory began as a "structuralist activity," to use Barthes's phrase. Structuralism in such fields as folklore and mythology grew out of an earlier phase of atomistic description. Dumézil's isolation of three Indo-European mythological 'functions' was preceded by encyclopedic works like Frazer's *The Golden Bough*. Propp's codification of a single set of narrative 'moves' in fairy tales followed upon the compendious assembling of motifs that culminated in Stith Thompson's *Motif-Index of Folk Literature*. Parry's articulation of a predictive theory for oral-formulaic composition was preceded, as we have seen, by decades of formula-collecting in Homeric and Germanic verse. As in these other structuralist approaches, oral-formulaic theory took a mass of surface data, posited a deep structure, and offered a scientific model for the transformation and realization of this structure. Oral-formulaic "singers" did not memorize a set text or a lexicon of poetic expressions but rather intuited systems for producing metrical utterances, generating them anew with each performance.

Structuralism was challenged on a collective front termed, inevitably enough, post-structuralism. A likely question to pose at this juncture, then, would be whether or not oral theory has entered a post-structuralist phase. Structuralist approaches have been attacked most often for being positivist and totalizing. Certainly the initial optimism of oral-formulaic theory in its claim to rigorously distinguish oral from written works has undergone a massive retreat. The hard edges of fixed epithets and formulas are softening into flexible strategies of various kinds. The poet as *bricoleur* (Lévi-Strauss's term, famously deconstructed by Derrida, 236), assembling the ready-made, has been displaced by anonymous tradition-dependence, in a move that parallels the post-structuralist one from the self to the subject of discourse. If "the death of the author is already inherent in structuralism" (Selden, 132; cp. Harris, "Nativist," 45), then oral-formulaic theory collaborated in killing off the poet, only to see him reborn in the 'singer' or performer. Recent work has followed the post-structuralist lead in displacing the poet still further with a network of intertextuality (Harris, "Intertextuality"). Further, oral theory has expanded to incorporate related fields such as speech-act theory (e.g. Quinn "Verse-Form"), while also acknowledging material conditions in a closer attention to the manuscript record of transitional literacy (O'Keeffe, *Visible Song*; Quinn, "Naming").

This monograph is intended as a contribution to the ongoing revision of oral theory. The first three chapters employ linguistics-based stylistic criticism and examine formulaic processes on progressively more complex levels. The first chapter starts with the most basic level of formulaic composition, that of *fixed formulas*, and investigates the applicability of Kiparsky's definition of "bound phraseology." Clemoes's recent work on Old English poetic language proves useful here. Hainsworth's speculations about *flexible formulas* provide the theoretical basis for the second half of the chapter. As a case study for these two levels of formulaic composition I examine what I term *syndetic formulas*, such as "habban and healdan," 'to have and to hold.'

In the second chapter I proceed to the level of the *system* (with reference to Fry's definition and subsequent modifications), and then to a level I term the *strategy*. My case study for this second chapter is the Old English *Rune Poem*. The unusually schematic nature of this poem provides a uniquely controlled environment in which to observe formulaic processes at work. My third chapter covers similar ground in examining the Old Icelandic poem *Alvíssmál*, and then proceeds to the level of the *theme* as practiced in *Völuspá* and the Eddic Atli poems.

I referred above to the lively critical dialogue that has addressed the application of oral-formulaic theory to the compositional practices of the

Old English poet. For the application to the Old Icelandic poet, however, the critical dialogue has progressed by fits and starts and has never been surveyed in detail.[5] To help remedy this situation I have included as my fourth and final chapter a survey of oral-formulaic criticism of Eddic poetry.

NOTES

1. For responses to Benson, see Russom, "Verse Translations" and Lord, *The Singer Resumes*, 117–20.

2. See e.g. Foley, *Traditional*, 5–8; and Lord, *The Singer Resumes*, 100.

3. Annual updates are made in Foley's journal, *Oral Tradition*.

4. See e.g. Harris, "Oral Poetry," 234: "The term 'Oral Theory' seems a desirable loosening of 'oral-formulaic theory' and is now ensconced in the most recent publications."

5. But see Harris, "Eddic Poetry," for a bibliographical introduction.

Revising Oral Theory

I

Fixed and Flexible Levels
In Syndetic Formulas

In his study of Homeric verse, Hainsworth redefines the formula as a "mutual expectancy of terms" (57) which, if compositionally useful, may coalesce into a strictly repeating *fixed formula*, but which may also occur in a more flexible representation. While neither occurrence is privileged, the critic may find it simplest to speak of a fixed formula sometimes acted upon by four processes: separation, inversion, expansion, and substitution. Most formulaic analyses of Anglo-Saxon verse, however, have tended to move quickly on to the next level, that of formulaic *systems*.[1] To apply Hainsworth's method directly, it is first necessary to reopen the investigation of fixed formulas.

A study undertaken in 1976 by Paul Kiparsky will provide the theoretical basis for the first part of this investigation. Kiparsky has suggested that formulas be compared to the "bound expressions" of ordinary discourse. In linguistic terms, bound phrases exhibit the following three properties: arbitrarily limited distribution, frozen syntax, and non-compositional semantics. The phrase "high jinks" is arbitrarily limited in that "jinks" can co-occur only with "high." The phrase "foregone conclusion" has frozen syntax in that it is not subject to internal transformations; i.e., the following sentence is ungrammatical:

*Your conclusion was foregone.

A phrase like "go the whole hog" has non-compositional semantics in that its meaning cannot be derived (except by etymologists) from its individual components. Kiparsky accounts for these properties by proposing that bound expressions are "listed whole in the lexicon"; that is, they behave as words rather than as phrases that can be broken into parts. In oral poetry, a fixed formula might behave in the same way.

I will apply these theoretical considerations to Anglo-Saxon verse in order to see 1) if fixed formulas exist, and 2) if they can be rigorously distinguished from other types of formulas. I will concentrate on syndetic formulas (defined below), expecially those which repeat within *Beowulf* and which are attested in several branches of early Germanic alliterative verse.

PREVIOUS LISTINGS FOR SYNDETIC FORMULAS

I am here proposing a new term, *syndetic formulas*, for formulas of the type "X and/or Y," e.g. "leofes ond laðes," ('lief and loath,' i.e., 'beloved and hated', Bwf 1061a, 2910a). In syndetic formulas, two terms (always the same part of speech,[2] often alliterating, occasionally rhyming) are conjoined in one half-line, usually by *ond*, less often by *oþþe*, *ne*, or *ge* ('and, or, nor, either/or') and occasionally by prepositions.[3] Semantically, these paired terms may be nearly synonymous (reduplicative phrases), e.g. "lað ond longsum" ('hateful and tedious'); contiguous (metonymic), e.g. "earm ond eaxle" ('arm and shoulder'); antonymous (contrastive), e.g. "ær oþþe sið" ('before or after'); complementary (suppletive), e.g. "wera ond wifa' ('of men and women'); or only vaguely related (enumerative), e.g. "heah ond horngeap" ('high and horn-gabled').[4] These last especially are likely to be nonce formations, a by-product of the Old English "appositive style," to use Robinson's phrase.

Examples of such formulas in Germanic poetry were catalogued quite early, in Sievers ("coordinierte substantiva," 465), Klaeber ("copulative alliterative phrases" and "riming combinations," xvi), Hoffmann's 1886 dissertation "Rime-Formeln im Westgermanischen," and Salomon's 1919 dissertation, "Die Enstehung der Zwillingsformeln." More recently, Geoffrey Russom compiled an unpublished list of examples from Old English and Old Icelandic poetry, which he has graciously allowed me to examine; Gurevic has published a list of examples from Old Icelandic (Eddic) poetry; and Clemoes (508–09) for Old English poetry. These scholars applied to "X and/or Y" formulas a wide range of terms. From Sievers's classification one could derive the term "coordinate formulas," which, however, sounds more mathematical than rhetorical. Klaeber's "copulative formulas" might equally well be found in the *Kama Sutra*; Hoffmann's "rhyme-formula" is too restrictive; "Zwillingsformel" or twin-formula, aside from sounding vaguely pediatric, is not very descriptive;[5] and Gurevic's "formulaic pair" seems a mistranslation of 'pair-formula.'[6] A few other Latinate possibilities (conjunct, conjunctive, and conjunctional) are either already used for other linguistic concepts, or sound like formulas that conjoin *other* formulas. The comparable term derived from Greek, "syndetic," is not as familiar, but has the proper rhetorical associations via *polysyndeton* and *asyndeton* (Klaeber e.g. applies the term *polysyndeton* to some lines from *Beowulf*, lxviii). The following definition of syndeton or syndetic construction from Hartmann's *Dictionary of Language and Linguistics* (230) should illustrate the suitable descriptiveness of the term for the present circumstances: "A construction, parts of which are linked together by means of conjunctions or joining words."

Syndetic formulas in *Beowulf* specifically could be sorted out from the formula lists in Watts's Appendix B. Russom's (unpublished) list is more useful, however; it is arranged alphabetically, excludes other kinds of formulas, and includes syndetic half-lines that do not repeat within *Beowulf*. Russom also cites syndetic formulas from Old Icelandic, and he includes non-alliterating syndetic formulas (e.g. *feorran and nean*). Hoffmann's lists, also, are admirably extensive and usefully organized. He presents the formulas in three ways: 1) according to which Germanic languages share them, e.g. Anglo-Saxon + Frisian + Old Saxon + Old High German; 2) by individual Anglo-Saxon poems, indicating which other poems share the formulas, e.g. Bwf + HbM + Sfr; and 3) by syntax ("coord. substantiva; coord. adj. and adv.; coord. verba"). Hoffmann also lists rhyming syndetic formulas (e.g. *frod and god*), and internally alliterating compounds (e.g. *felafrecne*). As such his work is probably the best all-purpose compendium of syndetic formulas, although it is not widely available. Meyer's list, also not very accessible, is derived from Hoffmann, but adds Old Icelandic examples. Gurevic's article aims at covering all Eddic "formulaic pairs," listing many examples and giving line references for the remainder. Clemoes's list is an (incomplete) index to Old English word pairs discussed in his monograph; it is classified by parts of speech. To supplement these lists I have consulted Bessinger and Smith's *A Concordance to the ASPR*, and *A Microfiche Concordance to Old English* (Venezky).

Listings for Germanic prose include Dorothy Bethurum's 1932 article, "Stylistic Features of Old English Laws," which lists alliterating and rhyming "legal formulas" (all syndetic). Hoffmann also cites from the Old English laws and from the prose of Wulfstan and Ælfric. More recently (in 1968), Inna Koskenniemi has catalogued a subset of syndetic formulas, those with synonymous elements ("reduplicative formulas"), in Old and early Middle English prose texts. I referred to these lists from prose in the hope that some common poetic formulas would prove to be proverbial or legal in nature.

A TEST CASE: *HABBAN AND HEALDAN*

The alliterating formula *habban and healdan* is one of a few oral-legal formulas that have survived into modern English, in the form "to have and to hold" of the Christian marriage vows.[7] Such a time-honored phrase is thus a likely candidate for the status of a fixed formula. Koskenniemi (134) cites a number of instances in Middle English, one in a marriage context: "habben & halden to wive" (*Seinte Marharete*, 6.13). Cleasby & Vigfusson, under "hafa," A.II.1, cites the cognate Old Icelandic phrase "hafa ok halda" from an unpublished deed (Dipl. i.6).[8] Klaeber (following Hoffmann) calls the phrase "West Germanic" (lxvi). Bethurum cites from the Old English laws "hæbbe and healde" (266),[9] and from Old Frisian laws "habba and halda," and "te hebbane and te haldene" (228). Hoffmann also cites two instances from Frisian, and five from Old High German (23), together with three citations from Anglo-Saxon prose, to which I have added a few other examples:

> habban ne healdan, Wulf. (Beth. 218.166)
> to hæbbenne & to healdene, Wulf. (Beth. 186.51)
> habban & healdan, Wulf. (Beth. 236.11)
> habban and healdan, BlH (Morris 55 [2x])
> habbað & healdaþ, BlH (Morris 55)
> to habbane & to healdenne, Bede (Miller 450.3)[10]

In Anglo-Saxon verse, the following half-lines occur, all of which will be discussed below:

MCh9 8	and hafa þæt feoh and heold þæt feoh
Bwf 658	hafa nu ond geheald
Bwf 2430	heold mec ond hæfde
Chr 1648	hafað ond healdeð
Dan 198	habban ne healdan
PPs 102.19	habbað and healdað
Mld 236	habban and healdan.

SEMANTICS OF *HABBAN AND HEALDAN*

In modern English the phrase "to have and to hold" exists, as far as I am aware, in no other form, and indeed in few contexts other than the marriage ceremony and, apparently, in legal deeds.[11] Its meaning is doubtless obscure to the modern listener, who is more liable to interpret "hold" as "embrace" (which results in an amusingly secular injunction). For modern English, any of Kiparsky's tests could be applied to the phrase. Its syntax is frozen; the phrase may not be inflected, inverted, or otherwise grammatically transformed. If "to hold" is used with its older meaning 'to keep watch over' (rather than simply 'hang on to'), then this sense is arbitrarily limited in its distribution; it must co-occur with "to have."[12] Or one may say the whole term has non-compositional semantics; in any case, the phrase is clearly a bound expression, and is marked as archaic.

It is of course more difficult to interpret the phrase as used a millenium ago. For one thing, its usage is likely to have varied from early to late Old English (from *Beowulf*, if the traditional dating is correct,[13] to *The Battle of Maldon*) and on into Middle English (*Seinte Marharete*). Since two of the citations are from *Beowulf*, one can at least apply a synchronic approach in those instances, examining *habban and healdan* in its contexts, in order to see if the phrase as a whole has a meaning beyond that of its individual constituents.

The first verse citation in the list given above is from the formally irregular *Metrical Charm* 9, a charm against theft of cattle. The larger context reads:

> and find þæt feoh   and fere þæt feoh
> and hafa þæt feoh   and heold þæt feoh
> [Mch9 7–8: and find that cattle and bring back that cattle and have
> that cattle and hold that cattle].

Formally this charm is only partly 'metrical,' which fact I suspect accounts for its using *habban and healdan* as an alliterative collocation operating across half-lines rather than within a syndetic half-line. But semantically the citation reveals what was probably the earliest usage for the phrase, namely in legal contexts. *Feoh* 'cattle' is the archetypal personal property; the word in fact can mean simply 'property' or 'wealth' (cp. the first line of the *Rune Poem*, "feoh byþ frofur," 'wealth is a comfort,' cited in the next chapter). We know from later and cognate citations that the phrase was used in deeds to convey a sense not just of owning ('having') property but also of retaining ('holding') it in one's possession. By echoing the language of law, the metrical charm aims not just at recovering the stolen property but also at regaining full, legal, inalienable possession of it.

As Clemoes has argued for the syndetic phrase *worda and weorca* ('by words and deeds'), an originally legal phrase can pass into verse and be "adapted to poetry's ways" (161). The uses of *habban and healdan* in *Beowulf* echo the legal use but develop it in a different direction. The first occurrence of the phrase in *Beowulf* takes place as Hroðgar is turning Heorot over to Beowulf. He enjoins Beowulf "to have and to hold" the hall:

> Næfre ic ænegum men   ær alyfde,
> siþðan ic hond ond rond   hebban mihte,
> ðryþærn Dena   buton þe nu ða.
> Hafa nu ond geheald   husa selest,
> gemyne mærþo,   mægenellen cyð,
> waca wið wraþum.

[Bwf 655–660a: Never before did I entrust the noble house of the
Danes to any man, since I (first) could lift hand and shield, except
to you now. Have now and hold the best of houses, be mindful of
glory, show great valor, keep watch against enemies].

The immediate context, then, is quasi-legal,[14] a temporary exchange of
sovereignty. Beowulf is to replace Hroðgar, as he who has "winærnes
geweald" (654a), control of the wine-hall. Hroðgar is not, however,
transferring the deed to Heorot over to Beowulf. The sense of *healdan* that
prevails here is not 'to retain' but rather 'to govern, watch over.'
Hroðgar's action reflects the larger context of many such exchanges of
sovereignty in the poem, including the illicit usurpations of Grendel, his
dam, and the dragon.

The next instance of *habban and healdan*, in fact, occurs in the larger
context of such a usurpation. Beowulf, like Hroðgar before him, has had
control of his own hall ("his sylfes ham," 2325) taken from him by a
monster, in this case a dragon. Before facing the dragon, Beowulf looks
back over his life, to the time when Hreðel 'held him and had him' as a
fosterling:

Ic wæs syfanwintre, þa mec sinca baldor,
freawine folca æt minum fæder genam;
heold mec ond hæfde Hreðel cyning,
geaf me sinc ond symbel, sibbe gemunde;
[2428–31: I was seven-winters (old), when the prince of treasures,
friend-lord of the people, took me from my father; Hreðel the king
held and had me, gave me treasure and feasting, was mindful of
kinship].

In the previous instance, *habban and healdan* took as object the
king's hall; here the object is one of the king's charges (Beowulf, his
fosterling) within the hall. In both instances the poet employed *habban
and healdan* within an overall context of an exchange of sovereignty. One
might next inquire whether these contexts associated with the syndetic
phrase *habban and healdan* differ from those associated with *healdan*
alone. In line 1182, Wealhþeow states that Hroþulf will 'govern

honorably' ("arum healdan") the young troop. Similarly, Finn vows that he will govern honorably ("arum heolde") a group of survivors (1099). Elsewhere, however, *healdan* takes a wider range of objects, from Beowulf's ship (296), the coast-line (230), and the hall (704), which Beowulf's men should have 'held' better against Grendel. In *Beowulf* the phrase *habban and healdan*, in contrast with *healdan* used alone, occurs in a more limited range of contexts: those having to do with a king's hall and his subjects within the hall. The *Beowulf*-poet makes a structural use of this constraint, by employing the phrase in two crucial moments where sovereignty is threatened. As a consequence, the bipartite aspect of the poem's narrative structure[15] (the parallels between Hroðgar and Beowulf as aged kings in crisis) is highlighted. There may even be an added elegance in that the second instance makes use of inversion (see further below).

The use of *habban and healdan* in *Christ* 1648 accords well with that in *Beowulf*, since its context is that of the (heavenly) lord ruling over his (angelic) subjects:

> Fæder ealra geweald
> hafað ond healdeð haligra weorud
> [Chr 1647b–48b: The Father of all has and holds dominion over the
> troop(s) of holy ones].[16]

The by now commonplace idea that the new Christian poetry 'converted' the heroic vocabulary applies well here, with the idea of sovereignty transferred to the "guest-hall" of heaven. But in the next two citations from religious verse, the conversion of sense is more radical, and any legal connotations lost. In *Daniel* the context reads:

> þæt hie him þæt gold   to gode noldon
> habban ne healdan,
> [Dan 197a–198a: that they would not have or hold that gold (image)
> as a god].

Here the phrase works within an idiom 'to have as a god,' rather than as a compound transitive verb with 'hall' or 'troop' as its object. The context in the *Paris Psalter* reads:

> Ealle his englas ecne drihten
> bletsian bealde . . . þa his mære word
> habbað and healdað.
> [102.16–19 All his angels bless, bold ones, the eternal lord . . . those
> who his glorious word have and hold].

In this instance, the sense of *healdan* that prevails is 'to observe, heed' (corresponding to the Latin *audiendam*).

Returning to heroic poetry, in its late incarnation in *The Battle of Maldon, habban and healdan* is used in the most literal-minded of ways, as but one of the many means in the poem to express the idea, "so long as he may have and hold [or wield] weapons" (236),[17] within no larger context of sovereignty:

> þa hwile þe he wæpen mæge
> habban and healdan.

Apparently the later poet of *The Battle of Maldon* no longer knows the earlier associations of *habban and healdan*. Clemoes, contrasting *Beowulf*, says that in *The Battle of Maldon* "this organic integration of society, warrior and weapons did not take place" (416). *The Battle of Maldon*-poet subsumes whatever resonances the formula might have had under a different stylistic system, the aim of which seems to be to express repeated actions (such as the wielding of weapons) in never quite repeated ways.[18]

Thus far, then, a survey of the poetic uses of *habban and healdan* reveals that the phrase did not have "non-compositional semantics"; the meanings of the individual components of the phrase were still perspicuous and available for use in different ways at different times and for different poetic purposes.[19]

ARBITRARILY LIMITED DISTRIBUTION

The two terms in *habban and healdan* are not arbitrarily limited with respect to each other; they each occur in a variety of other contexts. Since in *Beowulf* the terms co-occur only in this half-line formula,[20] their status differs from that of a habitual collocation (where the two verbs would 'cluster' together; see below). One other element of distribution, that of associated objects, was discussed above, and a purely grammatical constraint was not evident.

FROZEN SYNTAX

Habban and healdan does not exhibit frozen syntax. The more usual form is infinitival, but the phrase can be inflected for past tense, present indicative, and imperative. Inflection is probably allowable in any case within a bound expression, as in:

He went the whole hog.
I'm really gonna go the whole hog.

Kiparsky uses mostly noun-adjective combinations, e.g. "high jinks," "foregone conclusion," to discuss the grammar of bound expressions. Bound verbal expressions, such as *habban and healdan*, may act in another way. Consider the following: "wine and dine, wheel and deal, forgive and forget." The latter two expressions are perhaps most comfortably used in infinitival forms:

He really knows how to wheel and deal.
? I guess I just wheeled and dealt my way out of it.

It's time to forgive and forget.
? And so we forgave and forgot.

The first expression, however, may be inflected, and an object freely placed:

She really wined and dined me last night.
He wined me and dined me till the cows came home.

(For most speakers, the use of "wine" as a verb will be arbitrarily limited to this expression.) Furthermore, adverbials may be inserted:

We must forgive now, and forget.

Apparently, then, frozen syntax in verbal collocations does not exclude inflection, or insertion of objects or adverbials.

The order of elements within such phrases seems less subject to variation; most modern speakers probably do not generate utterances such as: *forget and forgive, *dine and wine, *deal and wheel, *learn and live, and so on.[21] No doubt the order is more likely to be fixed if a semantic progression between the terms is perceived: first one lives for a while, then one learns, etc. Notice, however, that the *Beowulf*-poet does invert the elements of the formula *habban and healdan*, in line 2430. This inversion may have been metrically conditioned, as "hæfde mec ond geheald" would be unmetrical according to the Sievers prosodic system.[22] Or we may have to do with a one-time poetic inversion for emphasis; cp. Kipling's "captains and the kings" versus the more usual "kings and captains."[23] In any case, the order *habban and healdan* far and away predominates. Order of elements thus far seems to be the most fixed characteristic of *habban and healdan*.

One other possibility to consider is that bound expressions may undergo a process of evolution. Limited distribution may develop more readily once a word takes on an archaic quality. In Modern English, for most speakers the word "jinks" has no meaning outside the phrase "high jinks," so it is hardly surprising that "jinks" exhibits "limited distribution." At the time of *The Battle of Maldon*-poet, the phrase *habban and healdan* as a whole might have had legal overtones, but it still had compositional semantics; *healdan* in the sense of 'watch over' could be used either within the formula or on its own. When such a meaning is lost in general, its presence within one phrase becomes anomalous, and speakers are forced to store the phrase "whole" in the internal lexicon. Before this semantic process takes place, however, a phrase might still have been "fixed" in other ways, most notably, again, in its order of elements.

OTHER SYNDETIC FORMULAS: INVERSION

Most of the recurring syndetic half-lines in *Beowulf* are fixed with respect to word order:

Bwf 40	billum ond byrnum
Bwf 160	duguþe ond geogoþe
Bwf 620	duguþe ond geogoþe
Bwf 1674	duguðe ond iogoþe
Bwf 2621	bill ond byrnan
Bwf 835	earm ond eaxle
Bwf 972	earm ond eaxle
Bwf 603	eafoð ond ellen[24]
Bwf 902	eafoð ond ellen
Bwf 2349	eafoð ond ellen
Bwf 698	frofor ond fultum
Bwf 1273	frofre ond fultum
Bwf 121	grim ond grædig
Bwf 1499	grim ond grædig
Bwf 1022	helm ond byrnan
Bwf 2868	helm ond byrnan
Bwf 1629	helm ond byrne
Bwf 2369	hord ond rice
Bwf 3004	hord ond rice
Bwf 134	lað ond longsum
Bwf 192	laþ ond longsum
Bwf 511	ne leof ne lað
Bwf 1061	leofes ond laþes
Bwf 2910	leofes ond laðes
Bwf 2571	life ond lice
Bwf 733	lif wið lice
Bwf 2743	lif of lice
Bwf 1048	mearum ond madmum

Bwf 1898   mearum ond maðmum
Bwf 2166   meara ond maðma
Bwf 1008   þa wæs sæl ond mæl
Bwf 1611   sæla ond mæla
Bwf 289   worda ond worca[25]
Bwf 1100   wordum ne worcum
Bwf 1833   wordum ond weorcum.

Some citations from other Anglo-Saxon poems and prose corroborate this order:

R86:6   earmas ond eaxle
Æl 448   frofer and fultum (prose)
BlH 201   frofre & fultomes (prose)
Sfr 112   wið leofne and wið laþne
Lay 1516 were him leof were him loþ (eME)
HbM 45   ne meara ne maðma
Mxl 87   mearum ond maþmum
Chr 917   wordum ond weorcum
Chr 1236 wordum ond weorcum
Glc 581   wordum ond weorcum
Glc 720   sceal ic his word ond his weorc
Glc 793   wordum ond weorcum
P104.23   worda and weorca
Phx 659   worda ond weorca
Rsg 7   ond min word ond min weorc
SFt 74   wordum and weorcum
Whl 84   wordum ond weorcum
XSt 48   wordum and wercum
XSt 222   wordum and weorcum.

Similarly, some cognate citations from other Germanic texts also corroborate this order:

Háv 35   liúfr verðr leiðr (OI)
H.6,9   liaf entha let (Fris.)

Hel. 1332	so lief so led (OS)
(OHG)	diu liebe und diu leide
Hel. 4369	grim endi gradag (OS)
Hel. (16x)	uuord endi uuerk (OS)
(OHG)	uuort ioh uuerk.

Other citations, however, occur in the reverse order:

R32:6	exle ne earmas
Æl 14	to fultume and to frofre
(OHG)	leid und lieb
Pra 64	hwile mid weorce, hwile mid worde.

Furthermore, some reversal is exhibited within *Beowulf* itself:

Bwf 137	fæhðe ond fyrene
Bwf 879	fæhðe ond fyrena
Bwf 2480	fæhðe ond fyrene
Bwf 153	fyrene ond fæhðe
Bwf 839	feorran ond nean
Bwf 1221	þæt ðe feor ond neah
Bwf 2870	ower feor oððe neah
Bwf 1174	nean ond feorran
Bwf 2317	nean ond feorran.

If fixed word order is to be a criterion for considering syndetic formulas as bound expressions, then these inversions might be evaluated in one of the following ways: 1) the given inversion is aberrant, or poetic. I argued as much for *habban and healdan* above, based on the predominance of the unreversed order; so one might argue also for the few inversions of *word and weorc*, *earm and eaxle*, *frofur and fultum*,[26] and *leof and lað* above. 2) The phrases under consideration are either a) not formulaic or b) not bound expressions, but rather chance collocations of two elements. This second line of reasoning might be employed especially if a "hard core of frequency" were not in evidence. "Fæhðe and fyrene" may represent such a case, since the phrase occurs only once outside

Beowulf (XSt 639 fæhðe and firne). An even more likely case is the phrase "cræft ond cenðu," for which Hoffmann cites only Bwf 2696. But Russom finds the phrase reversed in adjectival form ("cene and cræftig") in King Alfred's *Meters of Boethius* 10:51.[27] Given only two instances of the collocation, each the reverse of the other, one may reasonably suspect that neither a fixed formula nor a bound expression is involved.

There remains, however, the example of *feor and neah* versus *nean and feorran*. (Since Hoffmann cites only alliterating or rhyming syndetic formulas, the citations below are taken from Bessinger and Cleasby & Vigfusson):

A *feor and neah*

Bwf 839	feorran ond nean
Bwf 1221	þæt ðe feor ond neah
Bwf 2870	ower feor oððe neah
And 638	þam þe feor oððe neah
Phx 192	þonne feor ond neah
Phx 326	farað feorran ond nean
Jln 335	oþþe feor oþþe neah
WfL 25	sceal ic feor ge neah
Exo 1	Hwæt! We feor and neah
Gen 1047	feorran oððe nean
Gen 1029	se me feor oððe neah
Fms viii346	nær eða fjarri (OI prose)

B *nean and feorran*

Beo wið Geatas glæd,   geofena gemyndig,
nean ond feorran   þu nu hafast
[Bwf 1173–74: Be gracious to the Geats, mindful of gifts, from near and far you now have (them)].

Wæs þæs wyrmes wig   wide gesyne
nearofages nið   nean ond feorran
[Bwf 2316–17: The worm's warfare was widely seen, the cruelly-hostile one's battle, from near and far].

The evidence from frequency certainly supports *feor and neah* as the preferred order. One can even make an argument for poetic inversion in the second instance of *nean and feorran*, since "nean" neatly echoes "nearo" in the first half-line. The first instance is problematic since a lacuna may be involved (see Klaeber's note). Since the phrase occurs in an a-verse, one would think the poet could have begun with "feorran and nean" and then avoided the inelegant alliteration on "nu." In addition, this syndetic phrase does not alliterate, and so inversion would facilitate differing alliterative demands; a poet temporarily at a loss for an *n*-alliteration might well be led to an occasional, inelegant inversion.

I am not sure, however, that in modern usage inversion is not allowable. Does "near and far" sound thoroughly objectionable? The *OED2*, under both "far" and "near," cites only phrases with the order "far and near." There are at least two counter-examples from *Beowulf* which the *OED2* excludes. Cleasby & Vigfusson, under "nær," I, lists a cognate Icelandic phrase in the opposite order: "nær eða fjarri," glossed as 'nigh or far.'[28] The *OED2* under "nigh" lists the phrases "nigh and far" and OE "ge neah ge feor," the source of which is not given. Thus by a circuitous route one can find evidence for phrases in either order (given a conflation of neah, nean ['nigh, near'] etc. within one phrase-model).

Another possibly reversible syndetic phrase is *feond and freond*. The phrase does not repeat in *Beowulf* (and hence was not included above); it is found only in line 1864: "ge wið feond ge wið freond." It is found reversed, however, in Gen 2812 "þæs þu wit freond oððe feond," and in MB25:16 "freonde ne feonde." The similar modern phrase "friend nor foe" probably does not exhibit reversibility and thus provides no analogous evidence. This time both elements of the Anglo-Saxon phrase alliterate, so no argument from poetic usefulness can be made for the inversions.

Clearly, then, some syndetic phrases are reversible; hence the presence or absence of a fixed word order does not necessarily determine the bound character of a phrase. A fixed order, however, was the one Kiparsky criterion that most generally held true for syndetic phrases/formulas. Koskenniemi reached a similar conclusion for reduplicative formulas in Old English and early Middle English prose, where he found sixty-five reversible pairs, of which he says:

In spite of the changeable word-order they might be classified as set formulas, at least in a given linguistic period or literary genre. . . . Semantically, and morphologically, these word pairs resemble idiomatic phrases. They have reference to rather general ideas and are often linked by alliteration or assonance. Yet, the internal word-order of such combinations has not become fixed. (82)

SYNDETIC FORMULAS AND EXPANSION

One might expect that two terms paired in a syndetic half-line formula might also be paired in a collocation across half-lines.[29] Such an arrangement would prove economical for the *scop*, who needs both to generate half-lines and to link them alliteratively. However, for most of the repeating syndetic phrases in *Beowulf*, the paired terms exist only within the formula, and not also as collocations.[30] Two exceptions are "lað ond longsum" and "leof ond lað," which appear in the following combinations (a hyphen indicates co-occurrence in a half-line; a comma indicates collocation):

lað-long
- 134   lað ond longsum.   Næs hit lengra fyrst
- 192   lað ond longsum

leof-lað
- 511   ne leof ne lað
- 1061 leofes ond lapes se þe longe her
- 2910 leofes ond laðes

lað, long
- 83   laðan liges; ne wæs hit lenge þa gen
- 134   lað ond longsum.   Næs hit lengra fyrst
- 1061 leofes ond lapes se þe longe her
- 1257 lifde æfter laþum, lange þrage

long, lað
- 974   no þy leng leofað laðgeteona
- 2008 se ðe lengest leofað laðan cynnes

lað, leof
- 2467 laðum dædum, þeah him leof ne wæs

leof, long

    31   leof landfruma   lange ahte

    54   leof leodcyning   longe þrage

  1061   leofes ond laþes se þe longe her

  1994   leofes mannes, ic þe lange bæd

  3108   leofne mannan. þær he longe sceal

long, leof

  1854   licað leng swa wel, leofa Beowulf

  1915   se þe ær lange tid   leofra manna

long, long

   134   lað ond longsum. Næs hit lengra fyrst.

These examples appear to represent a collocative set for *l*-alliteration that variously makes use of three terms. Interaction with a number of systems and near-systems in *Beowulf* (labeled A–C below) further encourages this collocative set:

A   16   lange hwile

  2780   longe hwile

  1257   lange þrage

    54   longe þrage

    31   lange ahte

B 2591   Næs ða long to ðon

  2845   Næs ða long to ðon

    83   ne wæs hit lenge þa gen

   134   Næs hit lengra fyrst

  2423   no þon lange wæs

C 3082   þær he longe wæs

  3108   þær he longe sceal

  1061   se þe longe her

  1915   se þe ær lange tid

  2008   se ðe lengest leofað.

Frequency of occurrence argues for the following preferred usages: b-verses that use *long* adverbially (in three basic ways, via systems A, B, and C); collocation of these with *leof* and *lað*, individually or as paired in the syndetic formula. The less habitual usages are *leof* and *lað* in collocation (1x), and *lað* and *long(sum)* within a half-line (2x). On the basis of these hierarchies, I would propose the following interpretation of this collocative set. The poet has recourse to one highly traditional pairing[31] (*leof and lað*), and a schema for producing b-verses (using *long* adverbially). Since both these systems participate in *l*-alliteration, they lead to an intertwining, in which the half-line bond of *leof-lað* and the cross-caesura split of *leof-lað,long* are generally respected. I offer this interpretation, rather than one of expansion (see below), since *leof-lað* only 'expands' once, and *lað,long* only 'condenses' twice (and *leof,long* never).

BEARN-BRYD

The *Beowulf*-poet pairs *bearn and bryd* ('man and woman') in only one line (2956). But in *Genesis A*, these elements appear as part of a larger schema, which may involve some expansions of the Hainsworth type:

A *bearn-bryd*
    1062   bearn from bryde
    1119   bearnes be bryde
    2198   bearn of bryde
    2328   bearn be bryde þinre
    2539   bryd mid bearnum
    2765   bearn of bryde
A' *beorn-bryd*
    1813   beorn mid bryde
    2033   beorn mid bryde
    2639   bryde æt beorne
    2783   bryd to beorne
EXP A *bearn, bryd*
    1171   bearna strynan, Him bryd sunu
    1248   oð þæt bearn godes bryda ongunnon
    2186   æscod þæt me of byrde bearn ne wocon
    2534   bearn gelæde and bryd somed

EXP A' *bryd, beorn*
  1119   bearnes be bryde,   beorn ellenrof,
(EXP A) *bearn//bryd*
  2620   æðelinga bearn,   Ammonitare.
                       Gewat him þa mid bryde.

Earlier I cited a group of half-lines that may be schematized as "lif ond (wið, of) lice." This schema is meant to suggest that syndetic formulas bear a relation to formulas that conjoin two elements via a preposition. In the present example, an unparalleled syndetic half-line in *Beowulf* can be seen, via comparison with *Genesis A*, to be part of a system of lines schematized "bearn (ond/prep.) bryde." Hoffmann apparently considers one case to be an expansion upon this system; he writes Gen. 2532 (for 2534), "bearn . . . and bryd." Similarly, the other three lines grouped under EXP A might also represent expanded syndetic formulas.

In these citations the expansion occurs across half-lines, rather than across whole lines as was the case in Hainsworth's Homeric citations. But the Anglo-Saxon *scop*'s requirements are different from Homer's. The *scop*, who employs very few whole line formulas, finds it useful to have a stock of alliterating pairs to conjoin variously in the a-verse. Hence the tradition has generated numerous alliterating syndetic formulas. In one instance (*leof-lað,long*, discussed above), the *Beowulf*-poet intertwines such formulas with the other major set of poetic requirements, collocations. One may say that the *scop*'s grammar interacts with two *filters*: a metrical one, which encourages formulas, and a phonetic one, which encourages fixed alliterative collocations.[32] The examples from *Genesis A* provide even clearer evidence that two elements in a formulaic system can also occur within a collocative system. One may call the set of whole lines "expansions" of the set of half-lines, without, however, suggesting a hierarchy of either system (such also is Hainsworth's usage of the term). The idea of formular and collocative systems interacting, rather than expanding, is perhaps better suited to Anglo-Saxon practice. But my purpose has been to demonstrate that processes analogous to Hainsworth's expansions occur in Anglo-Saxon verse.

The sets of lines labelled A' and EXP A' all use *beorn* ('man') rather than *bearn* ('son'). As Fry has suggested ("Systems," 200), "near-homophones" seem occasionally to replace each other within systems; these lines in group A' may then be considered as variants within the system represented by group A. Additionally, in one line (1119, see the table above) *beorn* collocates with the "bearn-bryd" formula. This occurrence may be labelled as EXP A. In the final citation (lines 2620–21, [EXP A]), *bearn* and *bryd* occur in subsequent lines. The example is analogous to Hainsworth's most radical type of expansion, i.e., across the line break. Since a foreign name, "Ammonitare," intervenes between these two terms, one may hypothesize that the usual collocation was delayed. Or one may suspect that *bearn*, used in non-alliterating position in another common formula (*æþelinga bearn*), suggested its partner (*bryd*) from another system. Content alone did not necessitate the choice of *bryd*, since the poet has available other fairly interchangeable synonyms for "woman": *wif* (used 39x), *ides* (28x), and *cwen* (1x). The *Genesis A* poet, in fact, has an unusual fondness for employing the word *bryd* (29x). The interpolated *Genesis B* uses these synonyms: *wif* (11x), *ides* (6x), *bryd* (1x). *Beowulf* uses these: *cwen* (9x), *wif* (9x), *ides* (8x), *bryd* (4x). The *Genesis A* poet, unlike the others, has a half-line system that favors the use of *bryd*. As the scenario of expansion I propose here, however, is more freely speculative, I have parenthesized the label (EXP A).

The citations above exhaust all the lines from *Genesis A* in which *bearn-beorn-bryd* appear, and the discussion accounts for 17 of the 29 appearances of *bryd* via a system and its (proposed) expansions. The sampling is comparatively large, and provides good evidence from frequency; the interpretations can be cross-checked with the given ratios of occurrence. The pairing *bearn-bryd* appears as often within a half-line system as within a collocative system (4x, 4x). Allowing for the near-homophone *beorn*, however, the formular usage is double that of the collocative (excluding (EXP A) and EXP A'). The only time *beorn* interacts in a collocation (EXP A'), *bearn* and *bryd* are already paired in the a-verse. The only (speculative) expansion across the line break also involves *bearn-bryd*. The evidence from frequency, then, supports the preferred status both of the formula versus the alliterative collocation and of *bearn-bryd* versus *beorn-bryd*. (The one comparative example from *Beowulf* also supports both these hierarchies.)

HELM OND BYRNE

One final phrase I will consider is *helm ond byrne*, 'helmet and mail-coat,' occurring (variously inflected) in Bwf 1022b, 2868b, and 1629b. Russom cites from Old Icelandic *Hyndluljóð* 2 "hjalm oc brynio," which is paralleled in *The Waking of Angantyr* lines 44 and 96 (ed. Gordon). As a combining of two major (defensive) articles of weaponry, the phrase would seem to be of obvious use in martial poetry, along the lines of "billum and byrnum," 'sword and mail-coat,' Bwf 40a and 2621a ("bill ond byrnan"). More interestingly, the combining of the two terms often occurs (in *Beowulf*) across the line break, as noted by Watts (in her section "Brief Expressions," 252):

671b–72	isernbyrnan, // helm of hafelan
1290b–91a	helm ne gemunde, // byrnan side
2615	brunfagne helm, hringde byrnan
2659b–60a	urum sceal sweord ond helm,
	byrne ond beaduscrud
2811b–12a	goldfahne helm, // beah ond byrnan
2986b–87b	irenbyrnan,
	heardsweard hilted, ond his helm somod
3139a–40a	helmum behongen, hildebordum
	beorhtum byrnum.

Do these examples provide evidence of a flexible formula? The collocation is not alliterative, and even results in a rare crossed alliteration in Bwf 2615. Consequently we have not to do with two alliterating elements that would work equally well paired in a half-line or linked across half-lines (see the previous two discussions). The mutual attraction of these two terms is of another kind. Watts's comment on these lines is: "vaguely similar phrases and even some formulae are built by the listing of two or more pieces of armor" (252). She sees the lines in question, then, as related semantically more than formally, in their references to weaponry. The status of *helm* and *byrne*, however, is preferred. The sword-words (*bill, sweord* etc.) are more variable, there being more synonyms available. *Helm* and *byrne* are the elements that also co-occur in repeated half-lines, with Eddic parallels.[33]

At this point the individual critic's subjective appraisal takes over, but I think the evidence for *helm* and *byrnan* does support a fixed/flexible formulaic idea. A mutual expectancy of terms at times results in a formula, at times in adjacent or nearby occurrences. The one term seems to suggest the other, in a variety of ways, perhaps beyond the range, however, of Hainsworth's classifications. The two terms occur in too many positions to be readily schematized: on-stave, off-stave, in succeeding half-lines, and in succeeding lines. As is often the case in Anglo-Saxon poetics, it is difficult to see how this mutual expectancy is strictly speaking "compositionally useful." Moving from *helm* to *byrne* (and vice-versa in two instances) seldom provides the poet with a ready-made set of lines; and yet the formulaic associations of *helm ond byrnan* are so strong (or pleasurable) that the poet prefers building lines around this collocation.[34]

CONCLUSION

This chapter has examined all the repeating syndetic half-lines in *Beowulf.* Beginning with *habban and healdan,* it was shown that Kiparsky's tests do not apply to an expression that nonetheless seems idiomatic. In the absence of strictly linguistic criteria, then, the discussion relied on literary/critical methods to evaluate the status of the repeating half-lines.

For *habban and healdan,* parallels were noted in other Germanic texts (poetry and prose) and in modern usage, yielding a fairly clear indication that the phrase is a bound expression. In Old English practice, it was shown that the phrase could be inflected, and once, inverted. Two other syndetic pairings, *feorran and neorran* and *feond and freond,* seem to be idiomatic and yet reversible. For other cases, the reversing of lines seems to be either the result of poetic inversion, or evidence of a chance collocation, with frequency of occurrence a deciding factor.

Next the chapter examined the syndetic half-lines for evidence of expansion. Most of the terms paired in half-lines do not also occur in collocations or nearby co-occurrences. Three exceptions were considered, the first being *lað-leof, long,* where it was concluded that a syndetic formula is interacting with a b-line system, rather than expanding. The pairing *bearn-bryd* from *Genesis A* offered a better case for collocation as expansion; the idea of metrical and phonetic *filters* was suggested. One final case, *helm ond byrnan*, suggested a more radical expansion of non-alliterating terms, for which Hainsworth's concept of "mutual expectancy" seemed appropriate.

Based on these examinations, I would suggest that fixed formulas do exist, but statistical and literary/critical methods (as well as semantic analyses) are necessary for evaluating them. In a set of fixed syndetic formulas, the two alliterating terms are always the same and most often occur in the same order. They are conjoined most often by a simple conjunction and most often fill the half-line, with allowances for unstressed words particularly at the beginning of the half-line (see for example under *feor and neah* above). Half-lines in which the two terms are conjoined by variable prepositions, e.g. "lif and (wið, of) lice," might also be included in a set of fixed formulas.

To ascertain whether a syndetic half-line is formulaic but not fixed, one would look for systematic variation in one of the two terms. For instance, *hord ond rice* occurs twice in *Beowulf*, but these lines also occur:

912   hord ond hleoburh,   haleþa rice
1179   folc ond rice.

In the absence of many parallels suggesting the predominance of *hord ond rice*, one concludes that these half-lines are part of a larger system (as yet undefined), or else that the terms are paired in free variation.

Some repeated syndetic half-lines may nonetheless be non-formulaic except in a syntactic sense (i.e. in conforming to a syntactic frame such as 'noun *and* noun'). Alliterative poets were doubtless aware that they could easily generate half-lines by pairing two terms. A poet might even pair the same terms twice within a poem; but if other poets failed to do so, then the half-lines probably were not among the productive formulas of the tradition. *Lað ond longsum* may represent such a case; these half-lines are part of a rare set of repeated whole lines (Bwf 134 and 192).

Using this type of argumentation, and the evidence adduced above, I would characterize the following repeated syndetic half-lines as fixed and formulaic:

> earm and eaxle
> feorran and nean
> frofur ond fultum
> grim ond grædig
> habban and healdan
> leofes and laþes
> mearum ond maðmum
> sæla ond mæla
> worda and worca

and perhaps also the following:

> bearn (prep.) bryde
> fæhðe and fyrene
> lif (prep.) lice.

Hord ond rice may be part of a system, as may also *bill ond byrnan* and *helm ond byrne. Lað ond longsum* was discussed above; *eafoð ond ellen* may also be the *Beowulf*-poet's own coinage.

For non-formulaic syndetic phrases, one would look to the non-repeating half-lines. Some of these, however, would appear to be formulaic when cross-checked within the Anglo-Saxon corpus and with Germanic cognates, as in the following examples:

Bwf 2500	þæt mec ær ond sið
Ele 74	þonne he ær oððe sið
Ele 572	ne ær ne sið, etc. (11 other instances, plus 6 in reverse order)
Bwf 2269	dæges ond nihtes
Gen 2351	dæges and nihtes

| XSt 497 | dæges and nihtes |
| Exo 97 | dagum and nihtum, etc. (16 other instances) |

Bwf 279	hu he frod ond god
Wds 114	frodne ond godne
Ele 637	frodra ond godra

| Bwf 82 | heah ond horngeap |
| And 668 | heah ond horngeap[35] |

Bwf 656	siþðan ic hond ond rond
And 9	þonne rond ond hand
And 412	þonne hand ond rond.

Bwf 774	innan ond utan
Gen 1322	innan and utan
MB 30	innan and utan
Chr 1004	innan ond utan
Phx 301	innan ond utan
Gen 677	utan and innan
Sól 52	útan ok innan (OI)

| Bwf 1549 | wið ord ond wið ecge |
| Mld 60 | us sceal ord and ecg |

| Bwf 2472 | þa wæs synn ond sacu |
| Phx 54 | ne synn ne sacu |

| Bwf 1741 | weaxeð ond wridað |
| Gen 1532 | weaxað and wridað |

Bwf 993	wera ond wifa
Gen 1574	werum and wifum
Gen 2755	wera and wifa, etc. (many other instances)

Bwf 2395   wigum ond wæpnum
Mld 126   wigan mid wæpnum.

Syndetic half-lines in *Beowulf* not paralleled in Old English or Old Icelandic verse and thus most likely not formulaic would include the following half-lines:

1727	eard ond eorlscipe
161	seomade ond syrede
1337	wanode ond wyrde
2057	manað swa ond myndgað
2319	hatode ond hynde
600	swefeð ond snedeþ
1604	wiston ond ne wendon
1751	forgyteð ond forgymeð
1767	forsiteð ond forsworceð
2922	sibbe oþþe treowe
350	wig ond wisdom
308	geatolic ond goldfah
122	reoc ond reþe.

NOTES

1. This level of formulaic composition will be defined and examined in detail in the second chapter below.

2. According to Clemoes (156), syndetic half-lines in *Beowulf* occur about once every twenty-three lines, with approximately half of them being noun pairs, a quarter adjective pairs and the remainder verb or adverb pairs.

3. Thus also Clemoes, 155. Gurevic notes further that in such formulas the elements X and Y "occupy strong position in the meter" (33) and that they have the same inflectional endings (which is to say syndetic formulas operate syntactically as a unit). She also classifies syndetic formulas semantically, according to whether the pairing is based on opposition, complementarity or tautology.

4. See Clemoes, 156; Gurevic; and Koskenniemi, 90–94.

5. Fix, writing in German, uses the term "Zwillingsformel" in an article on syndetic formulas in Old Norse laws.

6. Clemoes does not settle on a term, but refers to binary collocations, couplings and word pairs (155–66).

7. The earliest version I have found in the wedding vows is from a Middle English fifteenth-century) addition to a Latin Manual: "I N[omen] take the N[omen] to myn weddid wyf [housbonde], to haue and to holde from this day forward" (Littlehales, 6). The *OED2* (under "have" B.I.c.) cites "to haue and to holde" from the matrimony section of the *Book of Common Prayer* (1549).

8. For Eddic verse, Kellogg's concordance yields only the full line "haldi Hel, því er hefir!," 'May Hel hold what she has [i.e. Baldr],' Ebr 5.

9. Cited in the Venezky concordance from Law II Cn 66.1 (the laws of Cnut, ed. Liebermann).

10. Further examples from Old English prose, including more distant collocations, can be found by searching the Venezky microfiche concordance. Thomas Hill has sent me a list of citations he obtained by computer, "using Gofer on the DOE file of OE prose," two of which from Ælfric indicate "a homiletic collocation which goes something like 'if he will not *hold* God's commands, then he will not *have* heaven's joy'"; the conditionality of the statement, or the wide separation of the two terms, may account for its 'reverse' order.

11. The *OED2* cites under "have" B.I.c. from Bouvier's *Law Dictionary* (1839–56): "The habendum commences in our common deeds with the words 'to have and to hold.'" For Middle English usages "in legal phrases," see the *MED* under "*haven*" v. 1a. (f), 'to possess and retain possession.'

12. The *OED2* glosses the whole phrase "to have (or receive) and keep or retain, indicating continuance of possession." Bosworth-Toller (Supplement) glosses the phrase as 'to have and keep' under sense A.II.2.b of "*habban*," 'to hold . . . under one's control,' which I think is nearer the mark in the Old English citations. Primary senses for "healdan" in B-T include 'to keep watch over,' governing such objects as a lord's thane or a guardian's ward (cp. the contexts below).

13. A mid to late eighth-century date for *Beowulf* was advanced most notably by Whitelock (*Audience*, 29–30) and generally accepted. The essays edited by Chase challenged this consensus but more recently Riedinger ("Relationship," 305), Fulk, Newton, and Clemoes (ch. one) have argued again for an eighth- or early ninth-century dating (see also Liuzza and Bjork & Obermeier). Clemoes builds a literary history around his arguments, such that *The Battle of Maldon* (which must date to after 991, the year the battle was fought) is regarded as more distant from the

traditional synthesis of language and world view seen in *Beowulf.*

14. Clemoes (44) suggest that Hroðgar's "coupling of finite verbs" (e.g. *habban and healdan*) here and in his 'sermon' (1741, 1751, 1567) is part of his hortatory style with overtones of vernacular preaching. But the same style is also found in laws, especially in the case of Wulfstan, who wrote both homilies and laws (see Whitelock, "Wulfstan," 224–26). On features of orality in Wulfstan's homiletic style, see Orchard.

15. See Chickering (19–23) and Shippey ("Structure") for surveys of opinion concerning the narrative structure(s) of *Beowulf.*

16. Translating 'dominion *over* the troop(s)' requires emending "weorud" to "weoruda," as a genetive dependent upon "geweald." In response to my query posted on the listserv ANSAXNET, James Earl suggested that "hafað ond healdeð" might operate in an *apo koinou* construction, governing both the object "geweald" before it and "weorud" after it.

17. Half-lines expressing the idea 'so long as he may wield weapons' are also found in Bwf 2038 and in an eleventh-century Old Norse runic inscription (see Page, 5–6).

18. On the formulaic variations in *The Battle of Maldon*, see Russom, "Artful Avoidance."

19. While my focus is on verse usage, an interesting Christian adaptation of the idea of property-holding occurs in the Blickling homilies and those of Wulfstan (see the brief citations above). Here the contexts relate variously to 'having and holding': the gospel in one's heart; spiritual fruit; belief in God's kingdom; rightness in one's heart; needful things in one's soul; and the likeness of God within us. Rather than secular property, the Christian should accept and retain the kingdom of God within. (In the one remaining prose citation, from the Old English Bede, the object of *habban and healdan* is *rice*, the secular kingdom or throne.)

20. The single exception is Bwf 2381, "hæfdon hy forhealdan," clearly a different sort of case, since "hæfdon" functions as an auxiliary.

21. Using the *OED2* on CD-ROM, I have found some quotations showing 'reverse' order: 'forget and forgive' under *comedy* n., *forget* v., *grudge* n. and *skirt* n.; 'dine and wine' three times under *wine* v.; and 'to hold and to have' once under *board* n. II.6.a in a marriage context from 1484 *Ripon Ch. Acts* (Surtees Soc.) 162.

22. For an accessible summary of Sievers's system, see Cassidy & Ringler, 274–88.

23. From "Recessional," 8 (I owe this example to Geoffrey Russom, and I thank Jack Kolb and Corinna Lütsch on the Victoria listserv for tracking down the reference). Cp. ME "kyngez and capytaynez," the alliterative *Morte Arthure* (ed. Hamel), 838. The *OED2* has later quotations in this same order under *Methusaleh* 2. and *secret* n. 3.a.

24. Clemoes (69) discusses how this pairing sums up "warriorship's essential combination of physical and mental power." He cites the nearly cognate Old Icelandic *afl ok eljun* and calls both phrases "a conceptual pairing . . . inherited from their Germanic ancestry."

25. Clemoes argues that the pairing of *word and weorc* "originated in legal practices and had already passed from there into poetic usage in Germanic antiquity" (161); cp. the discussion of *habban and healdan* above.

26.   This particular collocation has been discussed recently by Stephen Morrison. He concludes that in light of the usual religious contexts of the phrase, its use in *Beowulf* must likewise have spiritual overtones.

27. Clemoes cites this phrase as evidence that Alfred "clearly adopted a phrase he regarded as standard commendation of soldierly worth in the poetry he knew" ("Alfred," 216).

28. Cited under "fjarri," I, are two additional phrases, in contrasting order: "firr mér en nær," and "nær honum eða firr . . . mod., nær eða fjær."

29. Gurevic (46, citing Meyer, 293) notes a similar phenomenon in Eddic verse.

30. This assertion may be verified by consulting Lynch's *A Statistical Study of the Collocations in Beowulf*, or by cross-checking entries in Klaeber's glossary.

31. Cp. cognates and Anglo-Saxon parallels cited above.

32.   Patrick Conner has advanced a comparable notion of different "components." In a detailed analysis of *Beowulf* 702b–730a (Grendel's approach to Heorot), Foley discusses a variety of "traditional structures" underlying verse compostion, including recurrent syntactic frames (*Traditional*, 201–39).

33.   Gurevic (36–40) characterizes the Eddic examples as "military formulas," a subset of the semantically looser "complementary formulas."

34.   For slightly more flexible levels of formulaic composition, see Kintgen on "echoic repetition," and Ritzke-Rutherford on the "cluster." On the grouping of successive syndetic formulas in Eddic verse and two examples from *Beowulf)*, see Gurevic, 47–53.

35. The *Andreas*-poet may have borrowed this line from *Beowulf*; see Riedinger, "Relationship."

II

Flexible Formulas, Systems, and Strategies in the Old English *Rune Poem*

In a study that predates oral-formulaic theory, Adeline Bartlett catalogues the opening and closing "formulas" in a number of Old English poems. From the riddles of the *Exeter Book*, for instance, she cites (94) the line "Ic eom wunderlicu wiht," 'I am a remarkable creature,' which introduces riddles 19, 21, 25, and 26. Elsewhere she notes in passing that the *Rune Poem* follows the same pattern in describing each rune; the parallels are "essential and mechanical" (44). Poems that exhibit such "mechanical" repetitions provide, as I hope to demonstrate in this chapter, an unusually good opportunity for observing the interplay of fixed and flexible levels of formulaic composition.

FIXED AND FLEXIBLE FORMULAS IN THE *RUNE POEM*

The *Rune Poem*, an *abecedarium* for the runic alphabet, is unusual among Anglo-Saxon verse in that it exhibits a stanzaic structure. Most of the extant verse, lyric and narrative, is composed in long strings of alliterating lines, which editors sometimes divide into verse paragraphs.[1] A few other poems, such as *Deor* and *Wulf and Eadwacer*, suggest a stanzaic structure through their employment of refrains. The *Creed*, which paraphrases articles of the Latin *Credo*, and *Seasons for Fasting*, which comments upon observances throughout the liturgical year, are both composed in predominantly eight-line stanzas. Similarly, the stanzas in the *Rune Poem* may derive from special circumstances, in this case the unavoidably subdivided nature of an *abecedarium*. Each runic letter had as its name a noun beginning with that letter,[2] familiar examples being *þorn* and *æsc* ('thorn' and 'ash tree'), the two runes still employed to supplement the Latin alphabet in printed Old English texts. Each stanza of the *Rune Poem* offers up a few words of wisdom per rune name, running typically to three or four lines per stanza. For example, the first stanza, for *feoh* (the f-rune), begins "(feoh) byð frofur," 'Wealth is a comfort' (line 1a).

This opening line of the poem offers its first instance of a "mechanical pattern," in which may be observed processes analogous to the flexibility Hainsworth observed in Homeric formulas. This mechanical pattern occurs in the first half-line of each stanza, and may be schematized in this way:

(Rune name) *byþ* X,

where X usually corresponds to a noun or adjective.[3] This simple template resembles the "A is for apple" pattern common to many traditional English *abecedaria*. Furthermore, the use of "byþ" recalls the so-called "*biþ*-gnomes" of Old English wisdom poetry, as for example in *Maxims I* 80b, "Dom biþ selast," 'Fame is most excellent.'

An examination of all the stanzas in the *Rune Poem* reveals a certain limited flexibility in employment of this pattern. The rune name occurs as the first word in each stanza; its placement is not flexible.[4] The word *byþ* follows the rune name in 24 of the 29 stanzas, including the first six stanzas which make up the *fuþorc* section of the poem.[5] In five of the later stanzas, however, *byþ* fails to occur as the second word:

19   (gyfu) gumena byþ   gleng and herenys
     [Generosity among men is credit and honor]

22   (wen)ne bruceþ ðe can weana lyt
     [Bliss he enjoys who knows little of woes]

41   (eolhx)secg eard hæfþ oftust on fenne
     [The elk-sedge has its home most often in the marsh]

45   (sigel) semannum   symble biþ on hihte
     [Sun to seamen ever is in their hopes]

67 (Ing) wæs ærest mid Eastdenum
[Ing was first among the East-Danes].

The variations evident in these lines exemplify those types often observed in related formulas and systems, and further, the special types of flexible variation that Hainsworth describes. In line 67, for example, the variation involves verb tense. In most formulaic criticism, such variation is regarded as irrelevant for the purposes of formula equivalence; two half-lines that vary only in grammatical form count as "repeating" half-lines. Most of the runes name an everyday object or concept, which the poet describes in the "universal present" tense. But the rune name in this stanza, "Ing," exceptionally names a figure from the legendary past, and so the poet not surprisingly converts *byþ* and all succeeding verbs in the stanza into the past tense. Further, since *wæs* and *byþ* have the same metrical value, the poet was not obliged to depart from the predominating verse type (Sievers type A).

Line 41 likewise involves a change in the verb, from *byþ* to the equally functional verb 'hæfþ' ('has'). Line 22 substitutes "bruceþ" ('has' or 'enjoys') for *byþ*,[6] while the rune name appears quite exceptionally in the objective case (genitive, governed by "bruceþ"). For the substitution of the verb in these two instances one may compare Hainsworth's substitution within otherwise fixed formulas.

The overall function of the verb *byþ* and its variants becomes clearer if one compares the Scandinavian rune poems,[7] which are similar in structure to their Old English counterpart. In the Old Norwegian *Rune Poem*, a pattern of "(Rune name) *er* X" prevails (*er* meaning 'is'); but in five stanzas the verb is either "vældr" ('causes'), "gerer" ('gives'), or "kveða, köllum" ('they call, we call'). In the Old Icelandic *Rune Poem*, the opening pattern does not vary: "(Rune name) *er* (kenning)." Dickins (29–33) translates "er" as "=," by which one can see that in the Old Icelandic *Rune Poem*, in all three rune poems, in fact, the verb in the opening pattern is little more than a copula joining the rune name with its description. This opening pattern, then, can be defined somewhat more abstractly as "(Rune name) (copula) X."

The types of deviation from the pattern "(Rune name) (copula) X" exhibited in lines 19 and 45 correspond to two other types of flexibility as defined by Hainsworth. Line 45, "(sigel) semannum / symble biþ on hihte," employs *separation*, in which a formulaic pattern is split by the pressure of an intruding word. Here *byþ* is displaced to the next (half-)line, thus exemplifying the most radical type of movement discussed by Hainsworth. Presumably the poet could have chosen to write (or recite) the line "*(sigel) biþ semannum / symble on hihte," which would be both metrical (Sievers type "expanded D^a") and grammatical (cp. line 63, "(lagu) byþ leodum"). Perhaps the poet simply preferred the uninterrupted sequence of alliteration represented by "(sigel) semannum / symble." In both lines 19 and 41 the poet employs what Hainsworth would term *inversion* (of the *byþ* and X slots), although once again the poet's motivations are not readily apparent.

The author of the Old English *Rune Poem* begins twenty-four of twenty-nine stanzas with the strictly repeating pattern "(Rune name) byþ." Given such a high frequency of repetition, together with the fact that the pattern occupies the same location in each stanza, there can be no question of chance repetition. Consequently the *Rune Poem* offers us a more controlled laboratory for testing flexibility than does a poem like *Beowulf*, where some 84 per cent of the half-lines never repeat in the strict sense, and the remaining 16 per cent may repeat just a few times over the more than six thousand half-lines of the poem (Watts, 127). The special properties of the Old English *Rune Poem* also make it possible to characterize more confidently the few variations on this opening pattern. The kinds of variation that were observed in the five instances cited above accorded well with the Hainsworth types of flexibility: changes of inflection, substitution, inversion and separation. While one must make allowances for different genres, one may nonetheless feel a little more confident about identifying flexible formulas in poems less rigorously schematic than the *Rune Poem*.

I will cite one such example of formulaic expansion from the Old English biblical paraphrase *Daniel*. The half-line "metod mihtum swið," 'lord strong of might,' occurs six times in five Old English religious poems,[8] and is a likely candidate for a fixed formula. In *Daniel*, however, the following whole-line occurs (italics mine):

> 283 *"Metod* alwihta, hwæt! Þu eart *mihtum swið*
> [Almighty Lord, lo! Thou art strong of might].

It would seem quite likely that the poet knew the half-line formula as preserved in the other religious poems, and expanded it into a full line by means of a non-alliterating adjective ("alwihta"), an apostrophe ("Þu eart"), and the exclamation "hwæt," which readers of *Beowulf* will readily recognize as a traditional introductory exclamation. Indeed, this line from *Daniel* marks the beginning of "Azarias's hymn," which in another manuscript was recorded as an independent text.[9]

FORMULAIC SYSTEMS

For both Hainsworth and Fry the fixed formula descends from a more flexible prototype which, after generations of proven compositional usefulness, takes on a fixed shape. For Fry the prototype is the *system*, which he defines as:

> a group of half-lines, usually loosely related metrically and semantically, which are related in form by the identical relative placement of two elements, one a variable word or element of a compound usually supplying the alliteration, and the other a constant word or element of a compound, with approximately the same distribution of non-stressed elements. ("Systems," 203)

He then defines the formula as "a group of words, one half-line in length, which shows evidence of being the direct product of a formulaic system" ("Systems," 204). The Old English *Rune Poem*, in addition to providing evidence of *flexibility* in its opening pattern, also provides some unique evidence on the level of formulaic *systems*. Furthermore, the unique degree of schematization in the *Rune Poem* once again provides a more controlled environment in which to observe these formulaic processes at work.

As noted above, the pattern "(Rune-name) (copula) X" operates in the first half-lines of most of the stanzas, expanding in a few instances to the second half-line. An examination of other second half-lines in the poem reveals the repeated use of a formulaic *system* which can be defined as "(man-word)[10] *gehwylcum*":

    1b   fira gehwylcum [to each of men]
    7b   ðegna gehwylcum [to each of thanes]
    13b   rinca gehwylcum [to each of warriors]
    90b   eorla gehwylcun [to each of earls].

Fry's definition of the system adequately relates this group of lines; the alliterating element ("fira, ðegna," etc.) varies by means of synonymous substitution,[11] and the non-alliterating element ("gehwylcum") remains fixed. Drawing an analogy from linguistics, one may say that a substitution-in-frame or slot-filler model adequately describes the "grammar" of this system. Considering that each instance of the system occurs in the same part of a stanza (the second half-line), in an *equivalent site* as it were, then one may say the *Rune Poem*, in the lines just cited, provides a special proof for the validity of the slot-filler model of the system.

    Elsewhere in the poem, these similarly formed half-lines occur:

    2a   Sceal ðeah manna gehwylc [Ought however each of men]
    9a   manna gehwylcun [to each of men]
    43b   beorna gehwylcne [each of men]
    60a   sceal þeah anra gehwylc [ought however each of them].

The variations exhibited by these examples resemble those which were disregarded in equating fixed formulas: inflectional changes ("gehwylcum, gehwylc," etc.), and insignificant additions within the unstressed portion of the half-line (e.g. "sceal þeah," 'ought however,' a phrase often used to introduce gnomic lines). If one may disregard such variation for the purposes of system equivalence also, then this system need not be redefined to accommodate this second set of examples. On the basis of all eight half-lines, which occur in close proximity within a single poem, one may assert with much more confidence than usual the productivity of the "(man-word) *gehwylcum*" system.

Consider next these three verses (only the last of which, line 84b, occurs as the second half-line within its stanza):

12a and eorla gehwam [and to any of earls]
20b and wræcna gehwam [and to any of wretches]
84b and eorla gehwæs [and of any of earls].

Semantically, these half-lines are clearly related to those cited above, but another kind of variation is involved: the substitution of "gehwam" (or "gehwæs") for "gehwylcum," which resemble each other in sound and meaning, and which do not occur in the alliterating position (the more important position in Fry's definition). Presumably little thought was involved in this particular variation. One might express the "gehwam" substitution as an automatic consequence of the added use of "and" at the beginning of the line, revising this system model in the following way:

$$
(and)^a \left\{ \begin{array}{l} \text{fira} \\ \text{ðegna} \\ \text{rinca} \\ \text{eorla} \\ \text{manna} \\ \text{beorna} \\ \text{anra} \\ \text{wræcna} \end{array} \right. \quad \begin{array}{l} \text{gehwylcum} \\ (\text{gehwam})^b \end{array}
$$

Condition: if a, then b.

Alternatively, one might regard the "gehwam" lines as evidence for a more abstract system of the form "(man-word) (each-word)." Here, though, one begins to see a problem with the substitution-in-frame model, for one can no longer say which of the two elements constitutes the frame, and which represents the element substituted.

Consider next the following phrase, which occurs as a second half-line within the "eþel" stanza:

71b æghwylcum men [to every man].

This verse also bears a clear semantic relation to the half-lines already cited, but here the elements undergo inversion (and the "man-word" appears in the dative singular case rather than the genitive plural). Or are the other verses inverted with respect to this one? Or do all the lines merely represent a chance grouping of different ways of expressing the same idea? Once again, the fact that many of these lines occur in the same place in a stanza may indicate a felt equivalence among them; but one begins to encounter problems in the attempt to express such an equivalence via a surface model.

The problem becomes more acute if one attempts to relate the following verses, all of which again occupy equivalent sites (the second half-line position) within their respective stanzas:

> 77b elda bearnum [to sons of men]
> 81b eldum dyre [dear to men]
> 59b his magan leof [dear to his kinsmen]
> 55b æþelinga wyn [joy of princes]
> 74b deore mannum [dear to men]
> 10b ælcre spræce [for every speech].

In order to characterize all these lines by means of one surface pattern and a few types of flexibility, one might regard the first example as an optional conjunction of two man-words, rather than a man-word and an each-word. The second, third, and fourth examples could result from substitution of a more specific adjective ("dyr," "leof") or noun ("wyn") for the each-word, and the fifth example could reflect a combination of substitution ("deore") and inversion. The final example could be derived by substituting "spræce" for the man-word, with subsequent inversion (assuming that "ælcre" counts as a variant each-word, like "gehwam" above). In accounting for all these instances, however, this "flexible system" now relates "eldum dyre" ('dear to men') and "ælcre spræce" ('for every speech'), which otherwise one would not likely have thought products of the same underlying pattern.

Difficulties in relating these many solutions for one poetic problem stem in part from an inadequate theoretical base. In the years since Parry first wrote his definition of the formula, the substitution-in-frame concept of language has for the most part been replaced by generative, transformational grammars. The foregoing analysis has attempted to account for all the members of a system via "phrase structure rules," or surface descriptions.[12] However, even a deep structure grammar could not express a relationship between the last two verses cited above. This is not to say that surface-structure models have no validity; I have already shown how often the poet relies on the slot-filler system "(man-word) *gehwylcum*." But this mechanical system obviously interacts with the poet's non-mechanical linguistic and creative capabilities in ways too complex to define in terms of surface patterns alone. The slot-filler model acts as a *filter* on the poet's grammar, even as the alliterative and metrical requirements are filters.[13] If stylistic critics wish to describe formulaic composition on all its levels, they must rely not merely on mechanical schemas but also on somewhat more speculative intuitions, as substantiated by evidence drawn from literary-critical analysis.

FORMULAIC STRATEGIES IN THE *RUNE POEM*

The idea of *equivalent sites* offers one such method of analysis, suggesting that the lines cited above represent similar poetic solutions, even if collectively they transcend the level of a surface-defined system. Previously I related these lines via a "flexible system," but I would like to propose a more general term, *strategy*, for any non-mechanical yet demonstrably productive means of organizing material into verses within a formulaic tradition. One may then speak of an overall strategy underlying a great many of the whole lines that introduce stanzas in the *Rune Poem*. The strategy consists of an opening template followed by a system:

(Rune name) *byþ* X (man-word) (each-word),

where "X" usually corresponds to an appropriate noun or adjective, but occasionally to a prepositional phrase or even to an added man-word. (Since the "X" slot cannot be defined more strictly, I have throughout referred to an underlying pattern or template, rather than formula or system.) As demonstrated above, such a strategy would apply directly to the following lines:

  1   (feoh) byþ frofur fira gehwylcum
  7   (ðorn) byþ ðearle scearp ðegna gehwylcum
 13   (rad) byþ on recyde rinca gehwylcum
 84   (yr) byþ æþelinga and eorla gehwæs
 90   (ear) byþ egle eorla gehwylcun.

The following lines likewise employ this strategy, given the idea of a flexible system:

 10   (os) byþ ordfruma ælcre spræce
 55   (eh) byþ for eorlum æþelinga wyn
 59   (man) byþ on myrgþe his magan leof
 71   (eþel) byþ oferleof æghylcum men
 74   (dæg) byþ drihtnes sond, deore mannum
 77   (ac) byð on eorþan elda bearnum
 81   (æsc) biþ oferheah, eldum dyre.

The "nyd" stanza employs this strategy within the expanded domain of a hypermetrical line (italics mine):[14]

 27   (*nyd*) *byþ nearu* on breostan,
       weorþeþ hi ðeah oft *niþa bearnum*
       [Need is oppressive to the heart, yet often it is transformed for
       the sons of men].

In three other stanzas, the poet places the man-word in the first half-line, but drops the each-word:

 32   (ger) byþ gumena hiht
       [Spring is the joy of men]
 45   (sigel) semannum symble biþ on hihte
       [Sun to seamen ever is in their hopes]

63 (lagu) byþ leodum langsum geþuht
[Ocean is by men considered wearisome].

The "gyfu" stanza also employs a man-word in its first half-line, followed by two syndetic half-lines, and *then* by the "(man-word) (each-word)" system:

19 (gyfu) gumena byþ gleng and herenys,
wraþu and wyrþscype, and wræcna gehwam
[Generosity is among men credit and honor, support and worthiness, and to any of wretches].

The "elk-sedge" stanza portrays this razory plant (whatever its precise identity) in terms quite similar to the "thorn," but its victims do not appear until the sixth half-line, at which point the "(man-word) (each-word)" system is employed:

41 (eolhx)secg eard hæfþ oftust on fenne,
wexeð on wature, wundaþ grimme,
blode breneð *beorna gehwylcne*
[The elk-sedge has its home most often in the marsh, grows in water, wounds grimly, stains with blood *each of men*].

Four other stanzas relate the rune name, within the first two or three half-lines, to some group of men, but in no systematic fashion:

22 (wen)ne bruceþ ðe can weana lyt
[Bliss *he* enjoys, *who* knows little of woes]
48 (Tir) biþ tacna sum, healdeð trywa wel
wiþ æþelingas
["Tir" is one of the constellations, keeps faith well with *princes*]
67 (Ing) wæs ærest mid Eastdenum
gesewen secgun
[Ing was first among the East-Danes seen by *men*].

The remaining six (of twenty-nine) stanzas do not relate the rune names directly to groups of men. Interestingly enough, these rune names all describe some aspect of the world of nature: the ox and beaver, birch and yew, and hail and ice.[15] Apparently, the poet does seem to have something of a naturalist's (or encyclopedist's) eye for objects in their own setting.[16]

An awareness of this underlying strategy inevitably affects one's reading of the *Rune Poem*. Shippey remarks that the poet "sees his objects and abstracts very much anthropocentrically, according to how they affect people" (*Wisdom*, 20). But to a large extent this anthropocentric sense is conveyed through the frequently employed "(man-word) (each-word)" system. In the observation "(cen) byþ cwicera gehwam / cuþ on fyre, // blac and beorhtlic," 'a torch is known to living men by its blaze, bright and shining' (16–17), one might question whether the men have a meaningful role to play. Having so often begun with a formula that casts the whole stanza in a 'dative of interest' relation to some princely characters, however, the poet does seem to make the most of a formulaic opening. For instance, in the "torch" stanza just cited, the poet concludes "byrneþ oftust // ðær hi æþelingas / inne restaþ," 'most often it burns where princes are relaxing indoors' (17–18). There is no doubt that by the end of this stanza the torch has most effectively and pleasantly been brought into the world of the living. A similar case may be made for the "thorn" stanza, which begins "(ðorn) byþ ðearle scearp," 'Thorn is grievously sharp' (7), with the familiar "ðegna gehylcum," 'to each of thanes,' standing idly by in the second half-line. But by stanza's end these thanes are brought into much closer contact with the rune name, when the thorn is said to be "ungemetun reþe // manna gehwylcun / ðe him mid resteð" (roughly, 'quite nasty to anybody who sits down on one').

AN EMENDATION

An awareness of the stanza-introductory strategy in the *Rune Poem* may prove useful in interpreting the defective "peorð" stanza, which begins:

38   (peorð) byþ symble   plega and hlehter
       wlancum * * *   ðar wigan sittaþ

> [Chesspiece? is always play and laughter to proud * * * where warriors sit].

Dobbie's conjectural emendation (156) to the syndetic phrase "wlancum [*and wisum*]," 'for the proud and the wise,' suits the overall style of the *Rune Poem* well enough. A glance at other half-lines in the poem reveals in fact that the use of syndetic half-lines constitutes another quite productive strategy for the poet. The end of the "os" stanza (12), "and eorla gehwam / eadnys and tohiht," 'and to any of earls hope and happiness,' employs a syndetic half-line in conjunction with the by now familiar "(man-word) (each-word)" system. I have already shown how in the "gyfu" stanza the poet began with the "(Rune name) *byþ* X" pattern, added two syndetic formulas, and only then made use of the "(man-word) (each-word)" system. Might not a similarly expanded strategy have been employed in the present stanza? That is, after the syndetic formula in the second half-line, I suggest the original version next employed the "(man-word) (each-word)" system, as follows:

> (peorð) byþ symble   plega and hlehter
> wlanc[*a gehwylc*]um.

If the conjectural emendation aims at deviating as little as possible from the poet's usual practice, then surely "*wlanca gehwylcum" ('to each of the proud') offers the most appropriate solution, as compressed by haplography to "wlancum" somewhere in the transmission process. Such a compression, in light of the plethora of similarly constructed half-lines, might well be more understandable than the loss of a syndetic partner (Dobbie's "*ond wisum"), or a prepositional phrase (Dickins's "*on middum").[17]

AN INTERPRETATION OF THE "RAD" STANZA

One additional stanza deserves mention here for its problemmatic use of a syndetic half-line:

13   (rad) byþ on recyde   rinca gehwylcum
       sefte, and swiþhwæt   ðam ðe sitteþ on ufan
       meare mægenheardum   ofer milpaþas.
       [Riding is in the hall for each of warriors easy; but strenuous
       for him who sits above a powerful horse [riding] along the
       'milepaths'].

Most editors agree in separating "sefte" and "swiþhwæt" by means of a
comma, though the need for such a division within a syndetic half-line
would be unparalleled in my experience (see the many syndetic half-lines
cited in my first chapter). Editors have not, however, always agreed on the
interpretation of this stanza. Some favor a single meaning for "rad"; as
Shippey paraphrases, "riding is pleasant in prospect but hard when one has
to do it" (*Wisdom*, 20). Others have seen a pun on two differing senses of
"rad," either as 'music' versus 'horseback-riding,' or 'furnishings
(indoors)' versus 'furnishings (on a horse, i.e., a saddle).' (All meanings
besides 'horseback-riding' are otherwise unattested.)
        While I do not wish to add to "the fantastic structures already erected
on *The Rune Poem*" (Shippey, *Wisdom*, 19), nor to emulate those
Victorian commentators who could find a "membrum virile" lurking in the
most innocent-seeming of stanzas, I am surprised nonetheless that a sexual
double entendre has not been detected in these lines. A sexual connotation
for "rad" or "ridan" is not otherwise recorded in Old English, although this
fact is not surprising given the chasteness of most of the extant verse texts.
"Old English Bawdry" would fill a slim volume indeed,[18] with a few
riddles (to which I will return) constituting the most notable exceptions.
The *OED2* does record a meaning of 'to mount the female' for "ride" in
early Middle English,[19] and "ríða" has long been the euphemism of choice
in Iceland. Assuming for a moment that such a meaning existed or was
readily intelligible in Old English, and restoring to the syndetic half-line
its customary integrity, one can reconsider how the first two lines of this
stanza might have been perceived:

       Rad byþ on recyde   rinca gehylcum
       sefte and swiþhwæt   ðam ðe sitteþ on ufan

[Riding is, in the hall, to each of men soft and vigorous, for him who is mounted upon . . .].

The audience would be led to an indecorous conclusion, which however is denied them:

meare mægenheardum   ofer milpaþas
[a strapping good steed on the high-roads].

Only in retrospect would the audience now go back and supply the unusual break ('easy; but strenuous') within the syndetic half-line.

In implying and then retracting a risqué interpretation, the poet would be composing within a tradition attested by certain of the *Exeter Book* riddles, which despite their suggestive overtones yield 'proper' solutions such as "a (lock and) key," or "a butterchurn."[20] This interpretation arguably provides more literal glosses for the elements within the syndetic half-line.[21] "Sefte," usually glossed 'easy,' is now glossed 'soft,' recalling two other contexts in which "seft" describes a comfortable seat:

P88.3 7   ful sefte seld, þæt hi sæton on
          [very soft seats, which they sat on]
Glc 165   seftra setla
          [of soft seats].

Halsall translates "swiþhwæt" as 'strenuous,' to provide an antithesis for 'easy.' While the *Rune Poem* records the only occurrence of "swiþhwæt," the simplex "hwæt" (minus the intensifying prefix "swiþ-") usually translates 'vigorous, bold,' and in one instance refers proverbially to aggressive horsemanship:

GfM 81   Sum bið to horse hwæt
          [roughly, 'some people are daring on horseback'].

The cognate from Old Icelandic, "hvatr," can also connote aggressive riding, as in "ríða hvatan" (cited in Cleasby & Vigfusson); the related "hvatligr" translates 'brisk, active' and even 'manly.' Furthermore, the

Icelandic and Norwegian rune poems do not, as Halsall expresses it, "stress the strenuous aspect of horsebackriding" (112), but emphasize rather its pleasurable aspects for the rider, at the expense of the horse's labors:

> Reið er sitjandi sæla   ok snúðig ferð
>   ok jórs erfiði
> [Riding is joy of the rider and swift journey and toil of the horse],

or, as the Norwegian poem puts it, "Ræið kveða rossom væsta," roughly, 'Riding is hardest on the horse.'

THE STRATEGY OF INTENSIFIERS

As another strategy that the poet of the *Rune Poem* often employs, I will point to the use of *intensifiers* in alliterating position. Consider these three lines, each of which begin a stanza:

29   (is) byþ oferceald,   ungemetum slidor
       [Ice is very-cold, quite slippery]
71   (eþel) byþ oferleof   æghwylcum men
       [Homeland is very-beloved to all men]
81   (æsc) biþ oferheah,   eldum dyre
       [Ash-tree is very-high, dear to men].

Here the prefix "ofer-" 'very-' operates within the "(Rune name) *byþ* X" pattern to fill out the line metrically, and to provide an optional second vocalic alliteration. In another stanza, this strategy is used in conjunction with the strategy of syndetic expansion to fill out a whole line:

4   (ur) byþ anmod   and oferhyrned
      [Aurochs is ornery and 'overly-horned'].[22]

The fact that "ofer-" occurs in each case within the first line of a stanza, in what I have termed *equivalent sites*, provides added evidence for the genuine utility of intensifiers. In fact, there are many other instances in the poem of vaguely intensifying adverbs in alliterative position; for instance "*swiþ-*" and "*swyþe*," 'very,' 14 and 65; "*fela-*," 'very,' 5; "*ðearle,*" 'grievously,' 7; and "*miclun,*" 'muchly,' 2. To these may be added a host of other alliterating adverbs, "*oftust, symble, a, næfre, æfre, ærest, siððan,*" 'most often, frequently, always, never, ever, firstly, subsequently.'

THE STRATEGY OF COMFORT-WORDS

As one final, more generalized strategy, one may point to the fact that, as Shippey expresses it, "the runic poet shares with the gnomic ones a concern for comfort" (*Wisdom*, 20). In the first stanza the poet chose a word for comfort ("*frofur*") to fill in the "X" slot of the "(Rune name) (copula) X" pattern. To these comfort-words may be added a host of synonyms for 'honor,' that is, 'comfort' on a moral scale. Like the man-words, these vaguely benevolent terms provide a wide range of more or less interchangeable fillers for alliterating positions. This strategy, however, doubtless requires more deliberation than that of the intensifiers, and the comfort-words are in part conditioned by the morally gnomic aspect of the poem; things tend to be either pleasant or unpleasant in primers. The use of comfort-words, then, represents a slightly less useful, less automatic strategy, instances of which include the following lines (which also show the productivity of syndetic half-lines within the poem):

12b eadnys and tohiht [blessing and joy]

19b gleng and herenys [credit and honor]

20a wraþu and wyrþscype [support and worthiness]

21a ar and ætwist [help and subsistence]

24a blæd and blysse [prosperity and happiness]

28a to helpe and to hæle gehwæþre [as help and salvation]

38b plega and hlehter [play and laughter]

75b myrgþ and tohiht [mirth and hope]

85a wyn and wyrþmynd [joy and honor].

THE FUNCTION OF THE *RUNE POEM*

One final aspect to consider would be the probable reasons for the unusually schematic nature of the *Rune Poem*. A number of possibilities spring to mind: the poet may be incompetent (or uninspired); or the poet may be a beginner, and the poem a compositional exercise. The poem may be intended for children, or as a guide for beginning or amateur poets, or it may be kept simple to facilitate a mnemonic function; or it might to a large degree be folk-traditional, like the maxims.[23]

It may help to first examine this rune poem in conjunction with the three others edited by both Dickins and Halsall. The earliest of these, the Germanic *Abecedarium Nordmannicum*, occurs in the ninth century St. Gall MS 878, and consists of a brief bit of alliterating "mnemotechnical doggerel" (Derolez, xxvi), which may however be significant in that it links simplicity with the early stage of rune poems. In form it recalls the simple lists called in Old Icelandic *þulur*, which provide synonyms or names for various key characters or concepts: man, woman, plants and animals, kings, dwarves, ogres, and so on. Of these, the *Dvergatal*, or catalogue of dwarves, is perhaps the best known, since it appears embedded in *Völuspá*, and since names taken from it (including "Gandalf") surface in J.R.R. Tolkien's works of fantasy. The *þulur* provide an oral thesaurus and name list, and it has sometimes been claimed that they preserve one of the earliest forms of Germanic oral poetry.[24] In the introduction to his edition of the Old English poem *Widsith*, Kemp Malone has meticulously discussed how in that poem the bare *þulur* (of heroes and their tribes) were expanded into brief episodes, and thus provide the kernel for heroic narrative.[25] Similarly the *Abecedarium Nordmannicum* may represent an early, mnemonic form that the later poets embellished.[26]

The Old Icelandic and Old Norwegian rune poems represent stages of complexity intermediary between the *Abecedarium Nordmannicum* and the Old English *Rune Poem*. They may well belong to a period later than that of the Anglo-Saxon version, but like the Old Icelandic riddles and cosmological dialogues, they seem to preserve an older gnomic tradition. The Old Norwegian poem is composed in a skaldic meter, with the first line exhibiting a "(Rune name) (copula) X" pattern, followed by a second, rhyming line imparting some proverbial assertion about an obscurely related subject.[27] As an example, the first stanza reads:

Fé vældr frænda róge;
föðesk ulfr í skóge.
[Wealth causes strife among kinsmen; the wolf feeds in the forest].

The form of the first lines, and in a few cases the content also, recalls opening half-lines in the Old English version:

ON 10   Ár er gumna góðe
        [Harvest-time is good to men]
OE 32   (ger) byþ gumena hiht
        [Harvest-time is a joy to men]

ON 7   Hagall er kaldastr korna
        [Hail is coldest of grains]
OE 25   (hægl) byþ hwitust corna
        [Hail is whitest of grains].

The formal affinities between the Old English and Old Norwegian poems consist in the linking of traditional rune name associations with further gnomic material, which the Norwegian version, however, does in a more obscure fashion. Furthermore, the Norwegian version tends more toward kenning-like equivalences for the rune names, a tendency carried to completion in the Old Icelandic version.

The Old Icelandic rune poem is the most systematized of the four, employing in each of its stanzas the following schema (as illustrated in the first stanza):

(Rune name) *er* (kenning)   *ok* (kenning)
    ok (kenning)
(Latin gloss)   (king-word).

Fé er frænda róg   ok flæðar viti
   ok grafseiðs gata
aurum   fylkir
[Fee is strife of kinsmen and fire of the sea
   and path of the serpent
gold   king].

The verse form recalls the *ljóðaháttr* employed in the Old Icelandic riddles and cosmological dialogues; the first two half-lines alliterate while the third "full line" employs internal alliteration. The king-words, of which Dickins informs us (28) all but one are found in the extant *þulur*, all alliterate with the rune name; the incorporation of alliterating king-words is particularly noteworthy in light of the extensive dependence upon man-words in the Old English version. The "(Rune name) *er* (kenning)" pattern further recalls the opening line pattern in both the Old Norwegian and Old English versions.

Having outlined the stylistic bases of these other rune poems, I will now return to the Old English version and the matter of possible causes for its schematized style. One cause might be the poet's (putative) incompetence or comparative lack of skill. Geoffrey Russom ("Artful Avoidance") has discussed the *scop*'s level of competence in terms of the ability to go beyond absolute formulaic thrift, to not always employ the same formulas in parallel situations.[28] Russom shows how the poet-translator of the *Paris Psalter* alliterates "god" and "georne" several times in succession, with only minor variations. "Georne" 'eagerly' is an intensifier such as those I have noted in the Old English *Rune Poem*, and furthermore is not in the Latin version that the poet is translating; it simply represents one strategy that the poet repeated whenever a likely occasion arose. In contrast, the poet of *The Battle of Maldon* repeats parts of systems in a way that cannot be said to have facilitated composition; such repetitions seem rather to have been employed for aesthetic effect. How are we to assess the poet of the *Rune Poem* in these terms?

It should be clear from the variations upon the four basic strategies isolated thus far that the poet's method is not one of simple repetition. The "(Rune name) *byþ* X" pattern is used with the most regularity, but it undergoes occasional variation and can be viewed either as traditional for the genre, or as a means toward stylistic unity. The "(man-word) *gehwylcum*" system is perhaps used more often than might be aesthetically pleasing, but it should be noted that the use of such a formulaic system demands more skill than the mere repetition of formulas or alliterative collocations; the poet makes substitutions and even, as we have seen, generates similar lines that transcend a mechanical employment of the slot-filler system. For these substitutions, a prior knowledge of man-words alliteratively associated with rune names, such as the Old Icelandic version schematically provides for king-words, would have been particularly useful to the poet.

The intensifer strategy has also been shown to be more complex than the *Paris Psalter* poet's constant recourse to *georne* alone; the poet of the *Rune Poem* has a greater range of intensifiers and the choices cannot be termed automatic. Even the more skillful poet of *Beowulf*, however, employs *georne* in alliterating position in all four occurrences (lines 66, 669, 968, and 2294). No doubt the practice appears less offensive when employed sparingly as but one of many available strategies. In the case of the comfort-word strategy, the poet merely uses a thematically organized diction, drawing from a range of words that are related but not so strictly as to have been learned, say, from a *þula*. In reading over the less schematized parts of the stanzas, we observe that the poet has learned some traditional gnomic associations, devices associated with the description of natural phenomena and manmade craft items, techniques of expansion that produce hypermetrical lines, and a few sea-kennings.[29] While not approaching the rhetorical complexity of the "art poets," the poet of the *Rune Poem* has command of a few techniques, a limited range that is varied in a competent fashion.

In discussing the poet's competence, I have also theorized about the poet's training, and this consideration suggests another cause for the poem's schematic nature, namely in its possible origins as a beginner's exercise, as a work designed for the moral edification of children, or as a sample composition designed to instruct beginning poets in their craft. The first of these possibilities seems fairly unlikely since one would not expect a first attempt to be preserved; furthermore, the range of techniques evident in the *Rune Poem* suggests a poet who has been composing long enough to have acquired that range and a facility within it. The idea of a primer is more likely, and Dickins (v) claimed that the poem is "exactly parallel" to a nursery-rhyme ABC. Shippey (*Wisdom*, 19) worries that the poem might be too complex to have served as a basic primer, but he may be underestimating the medieval student's ability (and willingness) to memorize (we recall Alfred's reputed abilities in this regard),[30] particularly if the poem is intended to teach not just the *fuþorc* but also a bit of gnomic wisdom[31] and perhaps even some elementary poetic technique.

The latter function would seem to underlie the Old Icelandic and Norwegian versions, which are stripped of the descriptiveness of the Old English version; the Old Icelandic version in particular consists of little more than a list of kennings, with *heiti* (poetic synonyms) for kings added at the bottom of each stanza. We know that Snorri Sturluson, in his handbook for skaldic poets, saw fit to include catalogues of *heiti* and kennings arranged according to the concepts most useful in the poetry.[32] The manuscript of the Icelandic *Rune Poem* dates to two centuries after Snorri, and I suspect owes its preservation to a later interest in kennings, namely as clues for corresponding runes in the runic signatures of the *rímur* poets.[33] One may then seek corroborative evidence suggesting an instructional function for the Old English version.

Hugh Keenan has briefly discussed the reasons for believing that some sort of childhood instruction did occur:

> From Beowulf, it is evident that [children] were sent to board at foreign courts to learn necessary skills and graces if they were nobles. Besides feats of arms, they learned pithy words of wisdom . . . . Characters and narrators resort to such gnomic expressions throughout Old English verse. Perhaps they were instructed in such formal sentiments as children. (16)

He then suggests that the Exeter and Cotton gnomes are primers for such instruction. Blanche Williams (quoted by Keenan, 19) sums up a number of possible functions, saying that the gnomic poems "may have been used as a school exercise; perhaps for copy-books, perhaps for memorization, possibly as a model for alliterative compositions." She is referring to a later, monastic form of education rather than the common Germanic one to which Keenan refers, but presumably the governing principles for such model compositions would be similar.[34] One imagines that most aristocratic children, in picking up court skills and in memorizing the gnomes, would absorb some idea of poetic technique; not all of them would have been overnight successes like Cædmon and Alfred. Whether or not the *Rune Poem* was originally designed to offer instruction in poetic technique, I hope the poem has served such a function for those of us who, a millennium later, are still beginning students in the art of Anglo-Saxon verse-making.

NOTES

1. Precisely how the *Rune Poem* was laid out on the manuscript page is unknown, since the original has been lost; the sole witness of the text is the printed version in Hickes's *Thesaurus*. Halsall (27, 30–31), however, advances interesting arguments to show that Hickes's version may faithfully represent the stanzaic divisions of the original manuscript.

2. Two exceptions are *ing* and *eolhx* for the ng- and x-runes. As Derolez remarks, since "the sounds they stood for were never found initially, their names begin with another sound" (xviii).

3. Editors of the *Rune Poem* have not failed to comment upon this opening pattern. Dobbie (xlix) refers to the "almost uniform use of the *biþ* formula in the first line of each stanza," and Halsall (116) speaks of "the opening pattern characteristic of the majority of the stanzas in the poem: '*A* (rune name) *byþ B* (definition).'"

4. Whether the rune name or a runic letter began each stanza of the lost original manuscript is a matter of some dispute; see Halsall, 25–26. In either case, the rune name (whether written in by the scribe or supplied by the reader) must still be considered the first word of the stanza.

5. The first six runes apparently never varied in their order, and taken together give the Old English runic alphabet its modern name of *fuþorc*.

6. Halsall suggests the reason for this "break in the opening formulaic pattern" may be that "wen" or 'joy' "cannot be linked with an object or action—it is a subjective experience" (118). For a different interpretation of this half-line, see Stanley.

7. Cited below from Dickins, but see Lindroth for a fuller record of textual variants, and some remarks on the literary history of the poems. For additional bibliography, see Hermansson, 61 (under "Rúnakvæði" and "Rúnaþula"), and *Kulturhistorisk leksikon for nordisk middelalder* 21.307–08.

8. See Bessinger's *A Concordance to the Anglo-Saxon Poetic Records* under *swið*. The references are XSt 261, And 1207 and 1513, Chr 716, GfM 4, and Rsg 64.

9. On the relationship between these two versions, see Jones.

10. I employ the term "man-word" rather than "person-word" because most of the synonyms in the poem ('earls,' 'warriors') refer to (heroic) men specifically rather than people generally.

11. Fry in his own examples does not always observe this semantic equivalence; see Niles, chapter 5. Riedinger ("Formula," 306) prefers the term *set* for systems of formulas varying by synonymous substitution.

12. Recently some grammarians have been investigating "generalized phrase structure grammars," which however incorporate many of the insights of tranformational-generative grammars. For a collection of these approaches, see Jacobson & Pullum. Formulas appear to play a greater role in the acquisition of a second language, such as a traditional poetic language might conceivably represent; see Vihman.

13. See the discussion of filters in the previous chapter.

14. On the expansion of formulas into hypermetrical lines, see Nicholson.

15. Accepting the suggestion of Osborn & Longland, I translate the otherwise unattested "iar" (line 87) as 'beaver.' Other editors have suggested 'eel' or 'newt.'

16. Of course even if these stanzas do not employ man-words, one can sometimes sense that the world of man is not very far off; hence the yew-tree is termed "wyn on eþle," 'a joy on [one's] property' (37), and ice is a gem-like 'floor' (31).

17. Dickins, 16; first proposed by Grein (see Dobbie, 156).

18. See Magennis, 37–38.

19. See the *OED2* under *ride* v. B.I.3, with a citation from *The Owl and the Nightingale*, c. 1250.

20. In Dobbie, riddles no. 44 and 54; see also nos. 25, 45 and 62. The *Exeter Book* does not provide solutions, but the method of these obscene riddles is fairly obvious and is paralleled in other folk-riddles.

21. As for translating "sitteþ" 'is mounted upon,' I note that Toller adds a submeaning 'to ride' for "sittan." For the sexual meaning, I note that in Old English one could sit on other parts of the body besides one's 'sitter'; to sit on one's knees, for instance, was to kneel. In Old Icelandic "sitja á beð" could mean 'to lie in bed,' as in *Guðrúnarhvöt* 19 (Dronke, 20), "þá er vit á beð // bæði sátom," which Dronke translates 'when in bed we lay together.'

22. See Halsall (106) on the translation 'exceedingly horned' rather than the sometimes proposed 'having horns above.'

23. For a suggestion that the poem had a divinatory function, see Osborn (1981).

24. On the other hand, *þulur* have also been placed in a late, antiquarian phase.

25. Fry ("Widsith"), however, has opposed this view of the poem's development.

26. Halsall (42–43) points to a number of Latin *abecedaria* from which the poet of the *Rune Poem* may have drawn inspiration. Without positing a hypothetical *ur*-poem from which all the extant rune poems descend, it does seem likely that the similar introductory patterns shared by all the poems (as well as *Alvíssmál*, see below) indicate a Germanic tradition; see also Clunies Ross.

27. See Clunies Ross, esp. 27–35.

28. On the lack of thrift or economy in Old English poetry, see also Fry, "Variation and Economy."

29. The poet employs two kennings for 'sea,' "ganotes bæþ" and "garsecg," both in line 79, and one kenning for ship, "brimhengest" in line 66. For descriptive techniques found also in *Beowulf,* compare line 36, "heard, hrusan fæst," with Bwf 1364 "wudu wyrtum fæst," and line 30, "gimmum gelicust," with Bwf 1608 "ise gelicost" (see also Bwf 218, 727 and 985 and the discussion by Clemoes, 95). For techniques shared with the Old English riddles, see Sorrell.

30. In Asser's *De rebus gestis Ælfredi* par. 23 (ed. Stevenson, 20), we read that Alfred's mother offered to give a book of Saxon poems to whichever of her sons could most quickly learn the poems by heart. Alfred immediately went off with his master and memorized the poems. Recently Fry ("The Memory of Caedmon") has commented on this passage as it reflects memorial transmission of Old English verse; see my discussion of this point in chapter four. See also Berlin.

31. Hall argues that the poet intends not just to teach the runic alphabet but also "to suggest multiple aspects of the created world through wordplay and the use of comparison and contrast" (453). On the larger gnomic dimensions of the Norse rune poems, see Clunies Ross.

32. Later scribes appended additional *þulur* to the *Snorra Edda* (ed. Finnur Jónsson). I suspect the king-words appended to the Icelandic *Rune Poem* echo this interest in skaldic poetics, and are not intended, as Halsall maintains (37), to furnish alliterative 'clues' for the rune names.

33.   On these signatures, see Páll Eggert Ólason. A strictly comparable connection would not obtain for the Old English *Rune Poem* and Cynewulf's runic signatures, for these latter (insofar as we understand them) substitute simple rune names rather than periphrases (kennings) for rune names.

34.   It is interesting to note in this context the different forms of education that Alfred's children received. Æthelweard was educated in a "school of literary instruction," but Edward and Ælfthryth were brought up in court, where among other things they read and memorized "Saxon" poems (par. 75, Stevenson, 58–59). For an interpretation of this passage, see Bullough, 454–56.

III

Flexible Formulas,
Systems, Strategies, and Themes in
Old Icelandic Eddic Verse

In addition to the Old Icelandic *Rune Poem* discussed in the previous chapter, Old Icelandic verse provides numerous other opportunities to examine "mechanical repetition" on several levels from the half-line to the entire stanza. Unlike Anglo-Saxon alliterative verse, all the extant Eddic poems, the earliest of which are probably contemporary with Anglo-Saxon poems, exhibit an impulse towards stanzaic form.[1] Two of the poems usually judged to be the earliest,[2] *Atlakviða* and *Völuspá*, show some irregularity in their stanza divisions. Poems in the *ljóðaháttr* measure, however, follow a regular pattern of two alliterating half-lines, followed by a "full line" with internal alliteration. The poet then repeats this pattern to make up a stanza.[3]

FLEXIBLE PATTERNING IN *ALVÍSSMÁL*

The Eddic poem *Alvíssmál* is composed in *ljóðaháttr*, and, like the Old English *Rune Poem*, employs highly schematized stanzas that invite examination from the point of view of formulaic construction. Stanzas one through eight and the final stanza (35) provide a frame story: Þórr seeks to rescue his daughter from the dwarf Alvíss ('All-knowing'), and so detains him with questions (concerning the names or *heiti* for thirteen things), until the dawn arrives and Alvíss, we assume, turns to stone.[4] The central section, as Hollander suggests (*Edda*, 110), makes most sense

when viewed as a *heitatal* or catalogue of *heiti* (poetic synonyms), cast in
the form of a dialogue-poem between Þórr and Alvíss. The variations
made by the poet within the question-and-answer format are minimal to an
extraordinary degree, as illustrated in Þórr's first and ninth questions:

9   Segðu mér þat, Alvíss   —öll of röc fira
         voromc, dvergr, at vitir—,
     hvé sú iörð heitir,   er liggr fyr alda sonom,
         heimi hveriom í.
     [Tell me, Alvíss—all the fates of men I think, dwarf, that
     you know—how is *the earth* called, which lies before the
     sons of men, in each region?]

25   Segðu mér þat, Alvíss   —öll of röc fira
         voromoc, dvergr, at vitir—,
     hvé sá eldr heitir,   er brenn fyr alda sonom
         heimi hveriom í.
     [Tell me, Alvíss—all the fates of men I think, dwarf, that
     you know—how is *fire* called, which burns before the sons
     of men, in every region?].

The first half of each these stanzas is repeated verbatim, as is the case
throughout the poem in each of Þórr's 13 questions. Line 4, beginning the
second half of these question-stanzas, varies throughout only by the
insertion of the new concept-word (e.g. "iörð," the word for which Alviss
will give equivalent *heiti*), with the article ("sá, sú, þat, þau") declined
accordingly. In one of the question-stanzas (17), the concept-word "scý"
'clouds' is plural, and so the verb in the fourth half-line changes to the
plural "heita." Stanza 13:4 begins with "hverso" 'how so' in the *Codex
Regius*, but "hvat sá" 'what the' in later paper manuscripts, leading Bugge
to emend to the strictly regular "hvé sá" 'how the.' The line may be
allowed to stand, however, as the exception that proves the rule, as the
single instance in which the poet employed a minor variation. Taken
together, these fourth half-lines may be schematized thus:

     hvé (article + concept-word) *heitir/heita.*

These fourth lines vary from their pattern even less than did the introductory lines in the Old English *Rune Poem.*

The fifth lines within these question-stanzas vary to a more significant degree, but even these exhibit an added degree of schematization. As with the second half-lines in the Old English *Rune Poem*, this patterning takes place on the levels of the system and the strategy.

SYSTEMS AND STRATEGIES IN *ALVÍSSMÁL*

In the half-line that occurs fifth within each question-stanza, Þórr characterizes the concept-word in some way; the only pressing demand on the poet in these lines is to provide an alliteration for the concept-word. As in the Old English *Rune Poem*, however, the resultant half-lines vary much less freely than might be expected, given this single poetic requirement. Stanzas 9 and 25 have as their fifth lines:

9:5   er liggr fyr alda sonom [which lies for sons of men]
25:5   er brenn fyr alda sonom [which burns for sons of men].

These two lines vary only in the verbs "liggr" versus "brenn," a change governed by content rather than by form, since the noun "alda" carries the vocalic alliteration in each case. Stanza 27:5 reads:

er vex fyr alda sonom [which grows for sons of men],

but this time the changed verb ("vex") carries the alliteration. Three other stanzas employ an obviously related system, with 'sons of men' used as the subject of the verb rather than in a prepositional phrase:

15:5   er siá alda synir [which sons of men see]
31:5   er sá alda synir [which sons of men sow]
33:5   er drecca alda synir [which sons of men drink].

In stanza 13 "menn" is used instead of the periphrasis "alda synir": "sá er menn siá," 'which men see,' as also in stanza 23, "er menn roá," 'which men row.' These two lines could have easily been cast according to the above pattern, but again it is the comparative regularity that is remarkable. In stanza 21, the line "er liggia scal," 'which shall lie,' omits any mention of men. This line with its stress on the auxiliary "scal" is poor metrically; one may even wonder if "fyr alda sonom" dropped out somewhere in the process of transmission (especially in light of the parallel line in stanza 9, "er liggr fyr alda sonom"). Unrelated are the fifth lines of stanzas 17 and 19, "er scúrom blandaz," 'which are mixed with rain'; "er víðast ferr," 'which fares most widely'; and the two similarly constructed fifth lines of stanzas 11 and 29, "erakendi" 'born to the sea?' and "in Nörvi kenda" 'born to Nörr.' To sum up, six of thirteen lines are related by a slot-filler system, and an additional two by a related system. The remaining five lines are variously constructed.

Of particular note with reference to the rune poems discussed in the previous chapter is the fact that the eight related half-lines all employ man-words, and are paired with a half-line that introduces a varying concept-word or *heiti* (versus a rune name). Whereas the overall strategy for many stanza-introductory whole lines in the *Rune Poem* was:

(Rune name) *byþ* X   (man-word) *gehwylcum,*

here a predominant whole-line strategy is:

hvé (concept-word) *heitir   er* (verb) *fyr alda sonom.*

In each case the introductory half-line varies little, and the alliteratively linked second half-line employs a "man-word" system. The entire remaining portion of each of Þórr's question-stanzas in *Alvíssmál* (lines 1–3 and 6) is repeated verbatim.[5] I suggested above that the *Rune Poem* with its schematic structure may have served as a model composition for beginning *scops*. Similarly, Hollander suggests that *Alvíssmál* served "to impart for the use of skalds, in a form easy to memorize, a synonymic vocabulary of the *heiti* . . . of thirteen things" (110).

For the rune poems I presented additional strategies at work in the final portions of each stanza. Similarly, one can see repeated strategies at work in intervening answer-stanzas, in which Alviss provides five *heiti* (as used by five classes of beings, including men, elves, dwarves, etc.) for each of the "concept-words" from Þórr's questions. In each of Alvíss's stanzas, the first half-line conforms to a strict slot-filler system, in which the *heiti* of men are given:[6]

    10:1 Iörð heitir með mönnom [It is called *earth* among men]
    12:1 Himinn heitir með mönnom [It is called *heaven* among men]
    14:1 Máni heitir með mönnom [It is called *moon* among men], etc.

Most of the second half-lines within Alvíss's stanzas conform to the pattern visible in these examples:

    12:2 enn hlýrnir með goðom [but *heaven* among the gods]
    14:2 enn mylinn með goðom [but *moon* among the gods]
    16:2 enn sunna með goðom [but *sun* among the gods], etc.,

with the varying *heiti* carrying the alliteration. In the three stanzas where the *heiti* from the first half-line begin with vowels ("iörð," "eldr," and "öl"), the poet in the second half-line alliterates not on the *heiti* but on "ásom," 'the gods,' by inverting the system thus:

    10:2 enn með ásom fold [but among Æsir *earth*]
    26:2 enn með ásom funi [but among Æsir *flame*]
    34:2 enn með ásom biórr [but among Æsir *beer*].

The first whole line in each of Alvíss's answer-stanzas, then, is constructed with strict economy; further, the second half-line in these stanzas gives evidence that at least one formulaic poet consciously employed two slot-filler systems related to each other by inversion.

The second set of whole lines (half-lines four and five) in Alvíss's stanzas exhibits an economy nearly as strict. The basic underlying strategy shows up clearly in these examples:

    10:4–5 ígræn iötnar, álfar groándi
    12:4–5 uppheim iötnar, álfar fagraræfr
    16:4–5 eygló iötnar, álfar fagrahvél

18:4–5 úrván iötnar,   álfar veðrmegin,
        [(*heiti*) by giants, by elves (*heiti*)].

Here the names of beings (*iötnar* and *álfar*) provide primary vocalic
alliteration, while the *heiti* supply secondary alliteration in the first half-
line. In two cases, however, the *heiti* alliterate with each other, and then
"dvergar" ('dwarves') appears in the second half-line, presumably because
"álfar" is no longer needed to carry the alliteration:

14:4–5 scyndi iötnar,   enn scin dvergar
26:4–5 frecan iötnar,   enn forbrenni dvergar.

In the final half-line occupying this position, the second *heiti* is
monosyllabic, which fact may well have motivated the following
variation:[7]

34:4–5 hreinalög iötnar,   enn í helio miöð
        ['pure-liquid' by giants, but in hell 'mead'].

Remaining are the "full lines" in Alvíss's responses, the third and
sixth lines in his stanzas, where the meter requires internal alliteration.
These lines consist of a *heiti* and a class of beings (dvergar, Vanir, Æsir,
etc.) that alliterates with the *heiti*, either in apposition, or with the beings
in the genitive, or as preceded by the verb "kalla," 'they call.' Such a
pattern is best termed a strategy rather than a system, although it is worth
noting that "kalla (*heiti*) vanir" predominates in the first full line (eight out
of thirteen times), and "kalla dvergar (*heiti*)" and "kalla í helio (*heiti*)" are
employed in the second full line three and four times respectively.

In conclusion, *Alvíssmál*, like the rune poems, offers an unusual
opportunity to observe a poet's variations within a highly schematic formal
structure. This structure generates *equivalent sites* that make it possible to
group more confidently half-lines within systems, and lines and stanzas
within overall strategies.[8]

INTRODUCTORY FORMULAS IN THE *EDDA*

The other, less schematic poems of the *Edda* also employ "mechanical patterns" in what we may call, following Bartlett, *introductory formulas*. In *Völuspá*, the following lines all introduce a new stanza and a new element in the sybil's prophecy:

> 19:1 Asc veit ec standa [I know an ash-tree standing]
> 35:1 Hapt sá hon liggia [She saw an ax-handle lying]
> 38:1 Sal sá hon standa [She saw a hall standing]
> 64:1 Sal sér hon standa [She sees a hall standing].

In *Atlamál*, the following lines also introduce stanzas, and a new element in Kostbera's and Glaumvör's prophetic dreams:[9]

> 19:1 Örn hugða ec hér inn fliúga [I thought an eagle flew herein]
> 26:1 Á hugða ec hér inn renna [I thought a river flowed herein].

These six lines bear a systematic relation to one another, which can be schematized in this way:

> (Omen) 'I saw' [*hér inn*] INF,

where INF=Infinitive, and the adverbial "hér inn" is optional.

The lines from *Atlamál* come from a highly formalized subsection of the poem, in which Kostbera and Glaumvör recount the evil omens of their dreams, as they attempt to deter their husbands from an ill-fated journey to the court of Attila the Hun. For the majority of omens, the husbands offer benign, domestic interpretations. The patterned nature of this subsection, in which omen-stanzas alternate with interpretation-stanzas, offers a set of controls like those provided by the *Rune Poem* and *Alvíssmál*. Using the term introduced above, one can say that these poems offer *equivalent sites*, introductory half-lines in which repeated problems are solved in nearly identical ways. As with the *Rune Poem* and *Alvíssmál*, it is more likely that this sampling provides a meaningful pattern-with-variations than when the individual instances occur at widely spaced and irregular intervals throughout a poem.[10] This time, however, the sampling comes from a narrative rather than a gnomic poem, and so the implications for narrative poems like *Beowulf* may be more significant.

The introductory pattern in *Atlamál* and *Völuspá* regularly lends itself to A-type verses, with (Omen) providing the first arsis and obligatory alliteration, 'I saw' the first thesis, and (INF) the second arsis and thesis. In this respect, the pattern resembles that of the Old English *Rune Poem*. However, the three slots in this slot-filler model do not specify particular words, but instead require a "synonymous substitution" of the sort Hainsworth describes (82). For the first slot, the poet selects from a paradigm of omens (analogous to the rune names from the template discussed earlier). For the second slot, the paradigm consists of verbs of perception, variously conjugated and accompanied by a pronoun. In *Völuspá* stanza 38, other manuscripts have the variants "veit ec" 'I know' and "sér hon" 'she sees' for "sá hon" 'she saw,' which further indicates the interchangeability of these forms. An analogy can again be made with the *Rune Poem*, where the slot described as "(copula)" accommodates conjugational changes and substitution of various linking verbs. The third slot consists of an infinitive conveying the action of the omen; in *Atlamál* an additional adverb is employed ("hér inn"). One other line from this poem employs a participle in place of the infinitive:

> 17:1 Björn hugða ec hér inn kominn
> [I thought a bear *had come* herein].

To include this line, the template can be modified to read:

> (Omen) 'I saw' [*hér inn*] INF/PART.

The following line can be related to the template by invoking Hainsworth's concept of inversion:

> 22:1 Gorvan hugða ek þér gálga
> [I thought a gallows was built for you].

Here the INF/PART slot (*Gorvan*) and the (Omen) slot (*gálga*) exchange places (and a dative pronoun is incorporated in the unstressed portion of the line). Similarly, these next two whole lines can be related to the template via Hainsworth's concept of separation:

> 15:1–2 Blæio hugða ec þína   brenna í eldi
> [I thought your bedclothes were burning in flames]
> 28:1–2 Konor hugðac dauðar   koma í nótt hingat
> [I thought dead women were coming here in the night].

Here the INF/PART slot (*brenna; koma*) undergoes a radical displacement across the caesura, theoretically because some other word has "intervened." In this case the words are "þína" ('your') in the first example, and "dauðar" ('dead') in the second; in the latter especially one can see that a necessary adjective motivated the separation. In the first example, an additional formulaic association of *brenna* and *eldr* was probably at work, as evidenced in these half-lines from *The Waking of Angantýr*:

> 28   eldar brenni
> 111   eld brennanda
> 146   eldar brunnu.[11]

Syntactic evidence also indicates that this pattern operates across the caesura, for in these examples the second half-line completes a clause. In the case of the previous examples from *Atlamál*, the second half-lines that follow (not cited) either introduce a new action (17:2, 22:2, 24:6), or add an independent and formulaic adverbial expression (19:2 and 26:2: "at endlöngo húsi," "at endilöngo húsi" 'the length of the house').

One final instance of the template from *Atlamál* seems to combine two kinds of flexibility:

> 24:1–2 Blóðgan hugða ec mæki   borinn ór serc þínom
> [I thought a bloody sword was drawn from your tunic].

Here the (Omen) and (INF/PART) slots exchange places, as in stanza 22 above, but the (INF/PART) slot is also separated across the caesura, as in stanzas 15 and 28. By rearranging the pattern in this way, the poet achieves the obligatory alliteration. This hypothetical rearrangement, of course, may not necessarily reproduce the poet's thought process. The principal objection to a slot-filler model of composition is precisely that it does not adequately describe a speaker's grammar, as noted in the previous chapter. But there is formal evidence that all these lines were in some way "equivalent" (each begins a stanza and introduces the next dream element), and the slot-filler model economically describes variation within this equivalency. Again, one can say that the slot-filler model is a *filter* operating upon the poet's grammar. Schematizing a pattern-with-variations does not automatically reveal the poet's compositional strategies, but it does provide a plausible basis from which to speculate about such strategies.

For instance, in the final line cited above, perhaps the word "blóðgan" ('bloody') occurred to the poet predominantly (not first, necessarily), and the poet rearranged accordingly, utilizing both an underlying grammatical competence and a mechanical surface pattern. The variation may even be for effect, since the line introduces one of the last two, most pointed omens that finally silence Gunnarr's rationalizations. It is far less likely that all these examples represent simply a chance assortment of ways to express a given idea. The foregoing analysis considered all the dream stanzas in *Atlamál* and established the predominance of one pattern (based on seven instances, including those from *Völuspá*). The remaining instances were defined economically as variations upon this pattern (one inversion, two separations, and one inversion-separation). Since, then, this schematization is economical (or 'elegant') and descriptively adequate, there is no need to invoke random combination as an inelegant alternative.

In *Völuspá*, which does not share with *Atlamál* a regular alternation of dream and interpretation, but instead recounts its prophecies in a more compendious fashion, one finds at least one other way to express what I will call the theme of prophecy:

39:1–3 Sá hon þar vaða þunga strauma
        menn meinsvara

> [She saw wading there, through 'oppressive' streams,
> perjurous men].

59:1–3 Sér hon upp koma   öðro sinni
iörð ór ægi
[She sees come up, another time, earth out of sea].

In order to relate these lines within the overall pattern isolated thus far, one might argue in either of two ways; first, that these lines represent the kernel of the pattern, which was expanded to include the dream emblem in the first half-line. Conversely, one might argue that these lines represent a means to shift the dream emblem down to the next whole line, the alliteration then falling rather unusually on an adverb ("þar; upp"). As with the discussion of "blóðgan" above, however, the pattern for all the lines begins to expand beyond the point where it can be "mechanically" analyzed.

Contrary to Rogers's complaints, though, I see no reason why critics may not at this point proceed to indulge in what he calls "crypto-psychological" activity. Once the relationships among a group of lines extend beyond the limits of "elegant description," any proposed schema for the generation of such lines becomes speculative and unprovable. But such speculation may cast light on those aspects of any style, formulaic or not, which transcend the level of mechanical rearrangement.

THE THEME OF PROPHETIC DREAMS
IN EDDIC VERSE

Other Eddic poems incorporate dream stanzas, and employ introductory formulas quite similar to the template in *Atlamál*. Before examining these poems, however, a few words concerning the concept of a formulaic *theme* may be in order. My interest here is primarily in the relationship of themes to verbal repetition; I will not undertake to sort out the various distinctions between themes, motifs, type-scenes, essential versus decorative themes, and so on.[12] Parry wrote of a South Slavic poet that "the essential simple themes of the poem he learned with exactness and repeated faithfully" (450). Lord for his part noted that "the themes in the repertory of any singer tend to become more or less fixed in content in proportion to the frequency of their use."[13] Greenfield ("Exile") and Magoun ("Beasts of Battle"), who both in 1955 made the earliest application of the term "theme" to Anglo-Saxon verse, focused on the "formulaic expression" of such themes. In reaction to these two studies, Crowne emphasized the point that "the theme and the formula are distinct entities, and need not always coincide" (365). At about the same time O'Neil wrote that themes are "necessarily built of formulas, but most often and almost completely of formulas uncommitted to a single theme" (159; cited in Fry, "Themes," 50). Fry subsequently redefined the theme for Anglo-Saxon verse as "a recurring concatenation of details and ideas, not restricted to . . . verbatim repetition, or certain formulas" ("Themes," 53).[14]

Thus far the "theme of prophecy" has been signalled by a recurrent introductory formula. The point may still be made that most of the lines that follow this introductory formula are not committed solely to this theme. One must also take into account the more stanzaic form of Eddic verse, in which introductory formulas function something like the incremental repetition in ballads.[15] Nor is it yet clear whether all Eddic themes incorporate such introductory formulas, although I will provide a number of other examples later on in this chapter. From a comparative standpoint, one might note that a glimpse at Lord's various instances of the theme of letter-writing suggests that Serbo-Croatian poetry employs recurrent formulaic expressions to introduce its themes (*Singer*, 85). In the relation of themes to formulas, then, Eddic composition may resemble Serbo-Croatian more closely than Anglo-Saxon.

The theme of prophetic dreams includes some additional instances, the first from *Guðrúnarkviða II*, in which Atli dreams of the murder of his sons:

> 40:1–2 Hugða ec hér í túni   teina fallna
>   [I thought saplings had fallen here in the courtyard]
> 41:1–2 Hugða ec mér af hendi   hauca fliúga
>   [I thought hawks flew from my hand]
> 42:1–2 Hugða ec mér af hendi   hvelpa losna
>   [I thought puppies slipped from my grasp].

Here the poet begins not with the omen but rather the verb of perception, this verb being "hugða" in all cases. The template may be schematized thus:

> *hugða ec hér/mér* PP   (Omen) INF/PART,

where PP=Prepositional phrase. In the previous template from *Atlamál*, the phrase "hér inn" was inserted optionally; now a related slot (PP) has become obligatory in order to achieve a full-line template; further, the PP slot often accommodates alliteration. One sees this most clearly in line 40:1, where instead of "hér inn" the poet employs "hér í túni," with "túni" carrying the alliteration. Both lines 41:1 and 42:2 employ the phrase "mér af hendi," with "hendi" supplying one alliteration, and "hugða" another. In two other lines, the omen itself alliterates with "h," and so the poet makes an interesting variation within the template:

> 41:5–6   hiörto hugða ec þeira   við hunang tuggin
>   [I thought their hearts were with honey chewed]
> 42:5–6   hold hugða ec þeira   at hræom orðit
>   [I thought their flesh had become carrion].[16]

These lines may be schematized as follows:

> (Omen) *hugða ek þeira*   PP INF/PART.

By separating the PP slot across the caesura, the poet moves the object of the preposition ("hunang; hræom") into alliterating position within the second line. In one final instance from *Guðrúnarkviða II* the protagonist herself is the omen, and an expansion of the template across four half-lines occurs:

> 38:5–6   hugða ec þic, Guðrún,   Giúca dóttir,
>   læblöndnom hiör   leggia mic í gognom
>   [I thought you, Guðrún Gjúkadóttir, ran me through with a
>   venomous sword].

Here one may argue that the template interacts with another compositional strategy, namely building a whole line around the alliteration of a name and its patronymic. This is the only time such a strategy is employed in *Guðrúnarkviða II*, but the collocation clearly belongs to the tradition of poems about Guðrún.[17]

As with *Atlamál*, the foregoing analysis has accounted for all instances via a template and a few transformations of the Hainsworth type. This template is obviously similar to the one in *Atlamál*, but is expanded to operate over two half-lines. That the theme-introductory formulas used in these poems should be both related and yet distinct accords well with Lord's discussion of themes, in which he shows that different treatments of a theme distinguish different singers.[18]

We are fortunate enough to have preserved in *Völsunga saga* a prose paraphrase of the dream sequences in both *Atlamál* and *Guðrúnarkviða II*. This paraphrase offers further indications that the material in the poems varies according to a formulaic pattern, and does not represent a random assortment of ways to express the same idea. The prose version sometimes reproduces the poetic version exactly, but more often rearranges the sense in accordance with more usual prose syntax and vocabulary. I will let one clear example suffice. Recall that the most radical variation from the template occurred in the following lines from *Guðrúnarkviða II*:

> 38:5–8 hugða ec þic, Guðrún,   Gjúca dóttir,
>   læblöndnom hiör   leggia mic í gognom.

The corresponding line from *Völsunga saga* reads as follows (M. Olsen, 90):

> "Þat dreymdi mik," segir hann, "at þu legdir a mer sverde."
> ["I dreamed," he says, "that you struck me with a sword"].

One notes first of all that the saga-writer employs the much more common verb for dreaming, "dreyma." (In the entire paraphrase the verb "hugða" appears only once, the prosaic "þykkja" 'seem' four times, and "dreyma" the rest of the time.) The saga-writer also omits the apostrophe to Guðrún Gjúca dóttir, which as I argued above represented a poetic strategy. The elaborately poetic paraphrase for 'stabbing with a sword,' "læblöndnom hiör / leggia mic í gognom," is compressed into the direct, strictly prosaic assertion "þu legdir a mer sverde." We know that the writer of *Völsunga saga* is working rather closely with poetic versions, for stanzas are often cited between the prose narrations. And yet once the poetic restrictions are lifted, the saga-style reasserts itself in ways that make the formulaic rearrangements of the poetry all the more apparent.[19]

Another sequence of prophetic dreams occurs in a poem from the 'minor Eddic' canon, found not in the *Codex Regius* but rather embedded in the *fornaldarsaga* (or mythical-heroic saga) *Hálfs saga ok Hálfsrekka*. The poem, which I will call *Innsteinsljóð*, is edited as *Das Innsteinslied* in Heusler & Ranisch, *Eddica Minora*, 33–37. The three dream stanzas in the poem begin as follows:

> 7:1–4 Hálfr! dreymði mik— hyggðu at slíku!
> at logi léki of liði váru
> [Hálfr! I dreamed—think of it!—that fire blazed
> about our bodies]
>
> 9:1–4 Enn dreymði mik öðru sinni:
> hugða ek á öxlum elda brenna
> [I dreamed yet a second time: I thought fire burned
> at our backs]
>
> 11:1–4 Þat dreymði mik þridia sinni
> at vér í kaf niðr komnir værim
> [I dreamed a third time that we had gone down
> under the sea].

Only lines 9:3–4 relate directly to the template under consideration, and can be schematized thus:

hugða ek PP (Omen) INF.

The ninth and eleventh stanzas begin by employing the simple but common gnomic strategy of building half-lines around a sequence of ordinal numbers ("öðru sinni," 'a second time'; "þridia sinni," 'a third time').[20] All three stanzas, like the prose paraphrase in *Völsunga saga*, employ the prosaic verb "dreyma." This fact may suggest that stylistically *Innsteinsljóð* partakes somewhat of the prose that surrounds it; certainly the whole matter of differences in formulaic style between Eddic and pseudo-Eddic poems bears further consideration.

In addition to these extended dream sequences, the basic template associated with a theme of prophecy also occurs in a few isolated contexts. In *Lokasenna*, Loki and the gods exchange insults, some of which allude to the same misfortunes that were prophesized in *Völuspá*. Frey begins stanza 41 by conjuring up a vision of the Fenris wolf: "Úlf sé ec liggia / árósi fyrir," 'I see a wolf lying at the rivermouth.' If Loki does not cease his insults, Frey will bind him beside the wolf. In *Grottasöngr* 19, the giant-maids have a vision of calamity following Fróði's death; this stanza begins, "Eld sé ec brenna / fyr austan borg," 'I see flames burning east of the castle.' In stanza 16 of *Brot af Sigurðarkviðu*, Brynhildr recounts her dream of Gunnarr's death; she begins, "Hugða ec mér, Gunnarr, / grimt í svefni," 'I imagined, Gunnarr, a grim thing in a dream.' Here the template differs in its use of a substantized adjective and prepositional phrase instead of the "Omen INF" construction.

Hálfs saga ok Hálfsrekka preserves, in addition to the dream sequence in *Innsteinsljóð*, a wealth of prophetic stanzas, many of which employ a version of this template. King Alrekkr foresees for his unborn son, "ek sé hanga / á háum gálga," 'I see [him] hanging on the high gallows' (Heusler & Ranisch, 89). A merman warns King Hjörleifr of a Danish fleet, saying "Ek sé lýsa / langt suðr i haf," 'I see [something] gleam far southward in the sea' (Heusler & Ranisch, 90). King Hjörleifr and his crew already had a pretty good idea what was in store for them, for a talking mountain had risen out of the sea and recited this stanza (Heusler & Ranisch, 90):

> Ek sé Hringiu   haug of orpinn
> en Hera hníga   hvátinn spióti;
> sé ek Hiórleifi   haptbönd snúin,
> en Hreiðari   höggvinn gálga
> [I see a mound raised over Hringja, and Heri sink dead, run through
> with a spear; I see fetters wound about Hiörleifr, and a gallows-tree
> cut down for Hreiðar].

More distantly related contexts include *Hávamál* 70, in which the poet exemplifies a rather bald gnomic beginning ("Betra er lifðom," 'It is better to be alive') with the following vignette:

> eld sá ec up brenna   auðgom manni fyrir
>   en úti var dauðr fyr durom
> [I saw (hearth-)fires burn in front of a wealthy man, but outside the
> door was a dead man].

Similarly, many of the riddles of Gestumblindi are presented as a kind of vision; one (rather rude) riddle begins, "Hest sá ek standa," 'I saw a horse standing' (Tolkien, 81). Since, however, the template provides such a useful means of expressing perception, one should not be surprised to find it occasionally employed in literal contexts with no overtones of prophecy or envisioning. In *Hyndluljóð* 49, Freyja surrounds with fire the giant Hyndla, who observes matter-of-factly enough, "Hyr sé ec brenna," 'I see a fire burning.' Three other non-prophetic instances of the template will be dealt with in the following section.

THEMES AND THE QUESTION OF INFLUENCE IN *ATLAKVIÐA* AND *ATLAMÁL*

In *Atlamál* 38 (Dronke 36) a version of the template marks the moment when Gunnarr and Högni first catch sight of Atli's lands, in the line "bæ sá þeir standa," 'they saw the farmstead standing.' I will not attempt to force these lines into conformity with the theme of prophecy by invoking, say, the shared idea of 'boundaries' (between lands on the one hand, and dreams and reality on the other), although stranger things have been attempted in formulaic theme studies.[21] I think this line merely indicates the general usefulness of a pattern that elsewhere was adapted to suit a theme of prophecy. But this line is interesting for other reasons, for another poem on the same subject, *Atlakviða*, employs a similar line in the identical situation, in stanza 14, "Land sá þeir Atla," 'They saw Atli's land.'

Dronke (99) includes these lines among the "verbal echoes" that she claims indicate the *Atlamál* poet's familiarity with *Atlakviða*. But surely she is advancing a form of the old *Parallelstellen* argument for the influence of *Beowulf* on Cynewulf, for which formulaic theory provides an alternative explanation via the independent use of traditional formulas and themes.[22] In other traditions one often finds such moments of narrative transition marked by formulas or verbal echoes; one thinks of both the "hero on the beach" and the "traveller recognizes his goal" themes in Old English, or the "departure by horseback" system in Serbo-Croatian.[23] Outside the Atli poems I find one other likely instance of an Eddic (or pseudo-Eddic) "theme of arrival," in *Fjölsvinnsmál* 1.[24] This *Sleeping Beauty* analogue begins, in the extant version at least, with the arrival of Svipdag outside Mengloth's fire-encircled castle; this moment is expressed thus:

> Útan garða   hann sá upp um koma
>   þursa þióðar siöt
> [Outside the courts he saw rise up the residence of giant-folk].

Beyond their similar introductory half-lines, however, the "theme of arrival" in the two Atli poems diverges widely in treatment. *Atlakviða* is generally considered the more courtly; in this poem the heroes reach Atli's castle after a swift gallop through mysterious Murkwood. In the more provincial (perhaps "Greenlandish") *Atlamál*, the protagonists reach Atli's farm after rowing like mad across Limfjord.[25] In his discussion of themes, Lord writes of singers who are more adept at ornamenting a theme with set-piece descriptions (*Singer*, 78). Accordingly in *Atlakviða* 14 the poet goes on to list features of Atli's castle so exotic that later scribes comprehended them imperfectly at best (see Dronke, 54–57); we assume that the original audience, like that of *Beowulf* with its splendid descriptions of Hroðgar's hall, could appreciate such details of craftsmanship. In *Atlamál* 38, on the other hand, the lone architectural detail mentioned is a creaky gate outside Atli's farm.

It is possible, as Dronke's contends, that such widely divergent treatments might be the result of "deliberate artistic reworking by the later poet" (99), although her picture of a poet who conflated sources "in a deliberate, almost scholarly, fashion" seems to reflect a critic's reconstruction more closely than a poet's creation.[26] As with the

Parallelstellen argument, however, the likelihood of direct borrowing becomes more remote the more one discovers an unaccountably complex network of "verbal echoes" occurring within a wide range of poems. For instance, Dronke also points to *Atlamál* 80 (Neckel 83) "töggtu tíðliga / trúðir vel iöxlom," 'you chewed repeatedly, trusted well your molars,' as an echo of *Atlakviða* 37 (Neckel 36) "hiörto hrædreyrug / við hunang of tuggin," 'carrion-bloody hearts with honey chewed.' Apparently Dronke feels that the *Atlamál* poet deliberately passed up on such honey-coated delicacies in favor of an image suggesting "the coarse heartiness of Atli's eating, his mouth crammed" (136); for me the image evokes instead a dog gnawing on a bone with its back teeth). But I have already cited a closer echo of the *Atlakviða* line in *Guðrúnarkviða II* 41:5–6, "hiörto hugða ec þeira / við hunang tuggin," 'I thought their hearts were with honey chewed.' Is one to assume that this poem, too, is directly influenced by *Atlakviða*? Before doing so, one might wish to consider that *Guðrúnarkviða II* is probably contemporary with *Atlakviða*, rather than a later reworking, that it preserves in contrast with *Atlakviða* the tradition of a Guðrún who wreaks vengeance on her brothers rather than attempts to save them, that it shares with *Atlamál* on the other hand the use of a theme of prophetic dreams, and so on. One might well be led to conclude that the easiest route through this tangle of "influences" is via the idea of an independent reliance on traditional material and forms of expression.[27]

I will close with one other verbal parallel, which Dronke does not cite, but which seems to me another instance of a shared theme rather than a borrowing. In *Atlakviða* 33 (Dronke 34), Guðrún welcomes the returning Atli with a drink; the stanza begins, "Út gecc þá Guðrún," 'Then Guðrún went out.' In *Atlamál* 47 (Dronke 45), Guðrún goes out to welcome her brothers; this stanza begins, "Út gecc hon síðan," 'Then she went out.' Before claiming that the line is borrowed, however, one should consider that in *Brot af Sigurðarkviðu* 6, Guðrún also welcomes her returning brothers, in a stanza that begins abruptly, "Úti stóð Guðrún," 'Guðrún stood outside.' I expect the poet here could count on the audience to smooth over a rather abrupt transition via the familiar associations of a half-line that traditionally introduced a "theme of welcoming."[28] Another likely instance of this theme occurs in *Helgakviða Hundingsbana II* 42, wherein Sigrún is urged to welcome her husband (who has just emerged from his burial mound), with the line "Út gacc þú, Sigrún," 'Come out, Sigrún.' She even brings him a welcoming drink (st. 46), as Guðrún had done, and as was done traditionally by the valkyries when welcoming heroes to Valhalla (see Dronke, 68). Here we have an intriguing and profoundly evocative combination of themes, for these welcoming drinks may serve also as ironic reminders of the *erfi* drunk at funerals (cp. *Atlamál* 75, Dronke 72), and even the cup of marriage (for Sigrún lies down in the burial mound with Helgi, and Guðrún will soon murder Atli in his bed).[29] Recognition of such a skillfully handled interplay of traditional themes can only increase our appreciation for the thematic "tension of essences" under which the best formulaic poets both struggle and prevail.[30]

NOTES

1. Stanzaic form, combined with various types of alliteration, rhyme and assonance, also characterizes the non-Eddic verse (skaldic poetry, ballads and *rímur*), which however I will not be discussing here.

2. On the dating of Eddic poems, see Jónas Kristjánsson, *Eddas*, 26–30.

3. Stanzas infrequently run a line or two longer, particularly if a *þula* or name-list is interpolated. On the connotative uses of *ljóðaháttr*, see Quinn, "Verseform."

4. This assumption is based on other sources, e.g. the Eddic poem *Helgakviða Hjörvarðssonar* (sts. 12–30), in which a giantess is delayed until dawn and turns to stone. See further Acker, "Dwarf-lore."

5. These repeated sections are heavily abbreviated in the *Codex Regius*, although Neckel gives the text in full in his edition. See Harris ("Oral Poetry") on similar scribal abbreviation in *Helgakviða Hundingsbana II*, as discussed in my fourth chapter.

6. These *heiti* for men are identical with Þórr's concept-words; that is, Þórr asks 'what are the *heiti* for "iörð,"' and Alvíss answers, '"iörð" among men, but "fold" among the Æsir,' etc.

7. The more regular "álfar miöð" may have been rejected as too short; lines such as Háv 76, "deyr fé," exist but are rare.

8. For other discussions of the structure of *Alvíssmál*, see Güntert, Klingenberg, Watkins, and Acker, "*Alvíssmál*."

9. In one additional stanza, a second dream is introduced midway through, and the same pattern is employed: 24:5 "geir hugða ek standa," 'I thought a spear was standing'.

10. One of the objections raised concerning formulaic demonstrations has been that the putative parallels are often drawn widely from within poems as well as across generically different poems.

11. See also *Innsteinsljóð* 9:4 and *Hávamál* 70:1, both cited below.

12. For such terminological discussions, see Fry, "Themes"; Parry, xlii; Foley, *Traditional*, 333–34; Lord, *The Singer Resumes*, 156–57; and F. Clark, xxix–xxxi.

13. "Homer II," 440–41. Elsewhere, however, Lord writes, "The theme, even though it be verbal, is not any fixed set of words, but a grouping of ideas" (*Singer*, 69). More recently, in response to Fry ("Themes"), Lord has said of the "transitional" poetry in Old English: "It may possible be that the necessity that gave rise to themes with close verbal correspondence no longer existed or was felt" ("Perspectives," 21).

14. More recently Riedinger ("Formula") has shown that Old English formulas are context-sensitive, which is not, however, the same as showing that similar themes employ similar formulas.

15. Earlier critics had assumed an influence of the ballad upon a later stratum of Eddic poetry; more recently, however, Hughes and Vésteinn Ólason ("Ballad") among others have argued that the Icelandic ballad postdates the period of Eddic composition.

16. These two lines closely echo the scene they foretell as described in *Atlakviða* 36, in which Guðrún murders Atli's and her sons and then serves them to Atli as 'ale-dainties': "hiörto hrædreyrug / við hunang of tuggin," 'carrion-bloody hearts with honey chewed.' On the interpretation of such echoes between poems, see the final section of this chapter.

17. Kellogg's concordance (under Guðrún) cites Sgk I 10 and 15; Gðk I 16; Sgk II 7; HrB 14; Gðk III 2; Gðh 9; and Hmð 2. A similar strategy occurs in Old English verse; cp. "Wiglaf/Wihstanes sunu" in Bwf 2607 and 3076.

18. Lord, *Singer*, see esp. 78–94.

19. R.G. Finch examines other instances of paraphrase in *Völsunga saga*. He notes, for instance, "the substitution of a bald prose word or phrase for markedly poetic diction" (316), and the excision of "vocatives" (325).

20. Cp. Rgn stanzas 21 and 22; Grm 6–16; Vfþ 20–42; and Háv 147–63.

21. See Richardson's negative appraisal of the putative "hero on the beach" theme in Old English poety and elsewhere; cp. Griffith, 181.

22. For an intelligent review of this debate, see Shippey, *Verse*, 85–100; on Old Icelandic intertextual relations, see Harris, "Oral Poetry," 120–26.

23. See Crowne; Fry, "Hero"; G. Clark, "Traveler"; and Lord, *Singer*, 46–51.

24. Cited from Neckel's edition of 1914, since the poem, found outside the *Codex Regius*, is omitted from Kuhn's revised edition.

25. For these and other distinguishing features see Holtsmark, 14, as well as Hollander, 294 and Dronke, 99–107.

26. Not that there were no scholar-poets composing in the (late) Eddic period; one thinks especially of the monk Gunnlaugr Leifsson, who in the early thirteenth century translated Geoffrey of Monmouth's *Prophetiae Merlini* into *fornyrðislag* stanzas, and incorporated deliberate echoes of *Völuspá* (see Turville-Petre, 200–01). Oral-formulaic theory argues that shared formulas do not *necessarily* indicate a direct relationship between texts. One may still argue on other grounds for the influence of one poem on another, as Andersson ("*Atlamál*") does for *Atlakviða* and *Atlamál*.

27. A few reviewers of Dronke's edition expressed misgivings concerning her treatment of sources. Halvorsen writes, "The literary approach . . . can be of only limited use in the reconstruction of older stages in an oral tradition" (321), while Lönnroth writes, "What her editorial work needs is perhaps just a small injection of folkloristic and oral-formulaic theory to loosen up some of the rigidity of her philological and literary methodology" (56).

28. The theme of welcoming is probably reflected also in *Völundarkviða* 30, "Úti stendr kunnig / qván Níðaðar // oc hon inn um gecc / endlangan sal," 'The clever queen of Níðaðr stands outside, and (then) she walked into and through the hall.' The queen has seen Völundr approach, but instead of welcoming him, goes back inside to warn the king.

29. On funeral drinks, see further Russom, "Poculum Mortis." Such a substitution of the *erfi* for the welcoming drink may also be implied in Hamðir's ironic forecast of his (doubtful) return, in *Guðrúnarhvöt* 8. Of Jörmunrekkr's cup-brandishing in *Hamðismál* 20, Dronke notes, "he is drinking mockingly to their coming and ironically promising them [i.e. Hamðir and Sörli] splendid hospitality on the gallows" (234).

30. The phrase "tension of essences" is Lord's (*Singer*, 97), and was singled out for praise by Creed in "Preface," 21.

IV

A Survey of Oral-Formulaic Criticism Of Eddic Poetry

In their 1983 book, *Reading Beowulf,* Ogilvy and Baker characterize "the theories of the 'oral-formulaic' school" as one of three main critical movements of the past thirty years (160). More recently, O'Keeffe has written that "no single critical movement has changed the face of *Beowulf* scholarship more than oral traditional criticism" ("Diction," 89). Clearly oral-formulaic theory has become a fact of literary-critical history for Anglo-Saxon studies. The attendant body of criticism has been surveyed several times, most completely by John Miles Foley (*Theory*) and A. Olsen. Under these circumstances it is surprising that no detailed survey has been made for oral-formulaic criticism of Old Icelandic (Eddic) poetry,[1] especially since Eddic verse is often studied comparatively with Old English verse. The present survey is directed at filling this bibliographical lacuna, and intends also to document the new and profitable directions being taken by oral-formulaic criticism of Old Icelandic verse.

This survey will also chronicle the reception of oral-formulaic theory among Old Icelandic scholars. Oral-formulaic theory in its initial presentation, as found in the writings of Parry, Lord, and Magoun, sees formulas as a necessary by-product of the improvisational composition of oral epic verse. As is now generally admitted, however, formulas appear in other types of verse composed and transmitted in ways not accounted for by this model. Various Eddic poems may appropriately be classified as dramatic, gnomic or narrative, but not as epic. A well-known passage in *Egils saga* (ch. 59) indicates (for the skaldic poem *Höfuðlausn*) deliberative composition and memorial performance (to use Harris's terms), not improvised composition and performance. Furthermore, in the eyes of a few critics at least, some Eddic poems appear to be literary imitations or synopses of other Eddic poems. How then, can a theoretical model dependent on one set of compositional and performance factors be applied to a corpus where these factors are not in evidence?

One way to apply the oral-formulaic model has been to assume an *ur-* poetry for which these factors did apply. Germanic poetry of the Migration Period may have included orally improvised epics, which subsequently broke down into heroic lays. Formulas would then be an inheritance from this earlier era. One of the critics whose work will be discussed here, Andreas Heusler, vigorously opposed this model,[2] and scholars may well be skeptical of a theory based on an unverifiable foundation. One may instead wish to concentrate on the extant genres of Eddic verse and revise oral-formulaic theory to accommodate such genres, no longer insisting that formulas can arise only under the pressure of rapid improvisation. Stock formulas can appeal to poets working under many sorts of conditions.

This revision opens the door to an assertion like Sveinsson's that formulas are merely ornamental or fortuitous, scarcely worth emphasizing in contrast to a poet's original contributions. Here the undercurrent is one of distrust for the traditional craftsman as opposed to the solitary genius. It need hardly be pointed out that early medieval poets and audiences were unlikely to share this distrust. Nor can a poet's originality be judged before one has properly accounted for the use of traditional diction. Such a project should be considered no more damaging to the spirit of original genius than, say, the cataloguing of classical rhetorical topoi in medieval verse.[3]

Oral-formulaic theory has also been seriously challenged on the grounds that "oral" formulas exist in demonstrably "written" works. Such a dichotomy scarcely begins to account for the range of possible scenarios for composition and transmission in the mixed cultures of the Middle Ages, and critics have by no means agreed about what constitutes proof of orality or literacy. Yet one may well ask in what sense formulas are oral if they seem to occur in poetic translations or in literary imitations. One could of course employ a neutral term, formula, and describe its use irrespective of its ultimate origin. I have no unappeasable quarrel with such an approach, but I remain impressed (as Sveinsson was not) by the evidence of so-called pan-Germanic formulas (as well as the common Germanic alliterative meter). As Lönnroth will argue, such formulas are most easily explained as an inheritance from the common Germanic culture of the Migration Period, when there can be no question of composition in writing. It would be rather more difficult (and improbable) to account for all such formulas via a network of international, literary translators (although we know of a few such cases, as in the Old English *Genesis B* and its Old Saxon original).

Lastly, we must deal with apparent instances of literary borrowing, as when *Atlamál* is viewed as a secondary imitation of the primary heroic verse of *Atlakviða*. This approach has much in common with the book-prose approach to saga composition,[4] which at its most extreme sees every instance of a shared motif as a deliberate borrowing from a pristine, "classical" predecessor, usually by a late medieval hack with a decadent taste for the marvelous. The case of the Atli poems is controversial enough to merit separate treatment, which I have accorded it in the preceding chapter, where it was seen that some critics have argued against the claim of literary indebtedness. In other cases, such as the Helgi poems (as analyzed by Harris), the hand of a compiling scribe is more plainly in evidence.

BEFORE THEORY: RICHARD MEYER

Just as the work of Parry, Lord, and Magoun is anticipated to a certain extent by the formula catalogs of Schmidt and Sievers, so oral-formulaic criticism of Eddic poetry has its precursor in the formula catalog of Richard Meyer. Indeed, late nineteenth-century Germany witnessed a veritable industry of formula-collecting, as Meyer's bibliographical survey indicates (5–7).[5] Meyer's introductory discussion of how poetic formulas developed likewise anticipates oral-formulaic theory in some of its aspects. Meyer maintains that a poetic language developed out of everyday speech through a selection process governed by 1) suitability to a putative ritual function of the poetry, 2) metrical form, and 3) the literary taste of a given time, poet, or literary school. We can detect if we like something of Parry's "intimate connexion with metre" in Meyer's following hypothesis:

> Sobald die metrische Form sich genügend befestigt hat, kommt mit ihr ein zweites Kriterium für die poetische Verwendbarkeit des Sprachstoffs. . . .
> [As soon as the metrical form becomes sufficiently well established, there comes with it a second criterion for determining the poetic suitability of linguistic matter]. (9)[6]

Similarly, we may see something of the concept of formulaic systems in the following:

> Mit der strengeren Festigung der Form wird der Einfluss des bereits in den poetischen Vorrath aufgenommenen Materials auf den neu aufzunehmenden Sprachstoff immer grösser und der letztere wird in manigfaltiger Art nach der Analogie des ersteren umgewandelt.
> [As the form becomes more rigidly fixed, the material already accepted into the poetic vocabulary exerts an increasingly stronger influence upon newly adopted linguistic matter, with the latter transformed by analogy with the former in various ways]. (9)

One appreciates anew, however, the greater precision of oral-formulaic theory when realizing how vaguely defined are Meyer's "Sprachstoff" and "Einfluss." Nor does he make any connection with oral composition.

Meyer's vague theoretical framework carries over into his organizational principles, making his compendium something of a 'loose, baggy monster.' Consequently one finds poetic material classified in a great variety of ways: repeated verses, but also expressions of time, examples of anaphora, and refrains. Critics may with a good bit of rummaging find citations grouped in useful ways, although in general (as we will see) Kellogg's concordance provides easier access to parallel verses. But the formula collections of Meyer and his generation make at least one lasting contribution, namely the documentation of formulaic parallels not just within individual traditions but across all branches of Germanic alliterative verse. Especially in the wake of Benson's article, which suggested that Old English formulas may exist in literary compositions, many formulaic critics began to doubt the relationship between formulas and oral performance.[7] But if one discounts the unlikely prospect of later, extensive literary borrowings (while allowing for the likelihood of some independent evolution), at least some pan-Germanic formulas will have developed within the Migration Period as part of a shared, oral tradition.

HEUSLER AND THE ICELANDERS

Andreas Heusler in his *Die altgermanische Dichtung* (published in 1923) makes this same observation, while at the same time paving the way for its disparagement:

> Viele der einfacheren Formeln kennen wir aus Süd und Nord; sie können leicht urgermanisches Erbe sein, älteste Verse stabreimenden Stils.
> [Many of the simpler formulas are known from both the South and the North; they may well be an *ur*-Germanic inheritance, the oldest verses of the alliterative style.] (65)

Heusler prefaces this statement with a discussion of "Zwillingsformeln" (syndetic formulas),[8] and readily admits the traditional nature of such expressions which he asserts are unimaginatively employed in some of the 'lower forms' of verse ("niedern Gattungen," 164). But he considers as grossly exaggerated Kauffmann's contention (175) that the role of a poet is to recast material according to a restricted number of fixed formulas. Heusler regards formulas as a minor part of early Germanic poetic composition, far outweighed by the original contributions of the poet.

Heusler's observations became axiomatic for critics of Eddic poetry even down to recent times, and may be seen as underlying the few remarks that Einar Ólafur Sveinsson makes on the subject.[9] Like Heusler, he admits that a few word-combinations and collocations appear to be pan-Germanic, including such color-associations as 'red blood' and 'green grass.' He then refers to the more prevalent use of fixed epithets (or rather *sannkenningar*, since his whole discussion revolves around Snorri's term) in the poetry of Homer and in medieval ballads. Since, however, he feels that Eddic poetry exhibits more variation in this regard, he concludes that Eddic poems "intermingled less than is usual" for orally preserved poems. As an afterthought, he mentions the studies of Magoun and Lord, and Kellogg's dissertation (see below).

In selecting a few rather unprepossessing color associations from Meyer's formula lists (202–07), Sveinsson diverts attention from more significant pan-Germanic formulas, and indeed, from formulaic composition *per se*. Furthermore, in contrasting the use of fixed epithets, Sveinsson focuses on a Homeric feature that (as Whallon had shown in 1961) does not manifest itself to the same degree in Old English poetry; we need not be surprised to see Old Icelandic poetry more closely resembling Old English in this regard. And yet the direction of Sveinsson's argument (contrasting Eddic with Homeric verse, and then mentioning the studies of Magoun and Lord) leads the reader to place Old English in the Homeric camp, leaving Eddic poetry alone and unique on its North Atlantic island.

His later remarks on repetition confirm this isolationist tendency. Sveinsson considers that "the repetition of lines in describing like events" may well be "an ancient characteristic," and yet "one should be surprised that such features should not play a greater role in Eddic poetry than they in fact do" (162). The question of such repetition is dismissed before its significance within a theory of formulaic composition can be properly assessed.

Since Sveinsson's work appeared, two other Icelandic critics have attempted to reintroduce oral-formulaic theory. In 1980, Magnús Fjalldal presented a summary of Lord's *The Singer of Tales*, and promised a second article showing the theory's connection with medieval Icelandic literature. Such an article would have been particularly welcome, since most of the studies to date (which I will review shortly) have assumed rather uncritically the relevance of oral-formulaic theory to Eddic poetry. He also promised a third article presenting the contributions of Lord's followers, which might have helped prevent the needless repetition of objections (such as Sveinsson's regarding epithets) that have already been dealt with sufficiently in the critical literature.

Since Fjalldal was unaware of any previous summary, I assume he worked independently of Vésteinn Ólason, whose "Frásagnarlist í fornum sögum" appeared in *Skírnir* in 1978. Ólason summarizes *The Singer of Tales* as well as Propp's *Morphology of the Folktale*, but his interest in these theoretical works is in their application to the perennial problem of saga origins.[10] In this regard he is anticipated by Kellogg's observations in *The Nature of Narrative*, which he also summarizes. Ólason's work, then, is primarily a review article, yet he and Fjalldal deserve to be singled out as members of the younger generation of Icelandic critics who have been introducing the results of contemporary research in literary theory to a philologically-oriented academic stablishment.

ORAL-FORMULAIC THEORY: EARLY APPLICATIONS

In his pioneering application of the theory to Old English verse, Magoun had already noted that for "any comparative study of Old-Germanic formulaic diction concordances are equally needed for the Old-Norse Edda-type verse (*Eddukvæði* of Mod. Icel. parlance) and for the Old-Saxon corpus" ("Oral Formulaic," 459). Acting upon this suggestion, Robert Kellogg compiled a concordance of Eddic poetry as a Harvard dissertation in 1958.[11] In his introduction to the concordance, Kellogg undertakes a Magoun-style "formulaic demonstration" for *Sigurðarkviða in skamma* 1–6, and finds that "nearly sixty percent" of the lines in this passage are "matched either by formulas or by formulaic systems elsewhere in Eddic poetry" (11). He recognizes the problems inherent in interpreting this data, considering that Eddic poetry amounts to "roughly only a fifth that of Anglo-Saxon or Homeric traditional verse," that "the Icelandic poets had at their disposal a large poetic vocabulary," and that Eddic poems exhibit a "variety of age and subject" (6). He might also have mentioned the stanzaic qualities of the verse and the concommitant tendency to repeat large sections verbatim or incrementally within a single poem. These features would also tend to skew one's data, and may in fact indicate a different mode of formulaic composition and transmission, as later critics suggest.

Three years after Kellogg completed his concordance, Paul Taylor completed a dissertation on Eddic poetry and oral tradition under the direction of Magoun's former student, Robert Creed. Taylor's dissertation addresses many of the special considerations that must be taken into account in applying oral-formulaic theory to Eddic poetry, and yet his (unpublished) work has not entered the critical mainstream either. Taylor offers a formulaic demonstration for *Völundarkviða* 1–3 and notes that Eddic poetry displays a "significantly high proportion" (2) of formulas, despite the limited corpus available for comparison. Working in this early phase of formulaic criticism, he does not entirely avoid the pitfalls inherent in such formulaic demonstrations. Some of the half-lines he cites as formulas are paralleled only within *Völundarkviða* itself, which raises the objections mentioned earlier with respect to the special stanzaic qualities of Eddic verse. For other half-lines, Taylor cites "parallels" that share one of two words (e.g. "alvitr unga" and "váro unga"), which raises the sorts of objections Rogers and Whitman have made concerning comparable demonstrations by critics of Old English poetry. Nonetheless, especially in the charts later on in his dissertation, Taylor does provide convincing evidence of the formulaic habit in Eddic poetry.

Taylor also makes several interesting hypotheses regarding the written transmission of Eddic texts. He considers the poems to have been "oral in the very special sense of composition *in* performance by a trained singer" (1), that is, he accepts Parry and Lord's model of an improvising "singer of tales." And yet he recognizes that the few texts extant in more than one version "are identical, except for insignificant orthographic variations" (82),[12] which he regards as symptomatic of "literary copying rather than several different dictations" (83). He also sees as evidence of literary "tampering" a number of incomplete lines and misplaced stanzas, "each of which suggests that literary transmission of the poems or faulty memorization of the texts have caused irrevocable corruptions of earlier oral forms" (83). As we will see, Lönnroth will also propose an influence of memorization upon the transmission of Eddic texts, but Taylor's model, assuming "oral performance in the ninth century" (83) for the oldest poems, better accounts for the at least partial reliance upon formulas that the present texts exhibit. Furthermore, Taylor suggests that the "block repetitions" exhibited by some poems reflect the "literary polishing of oral texts" (83), that the scribe strictly regularizes passages where the singer had only approached verbatim repetition. Taylor asserts that there probably was a century-long gap between the active composition of Eddic texts and their written preservation; presumably he would agree that some of the "polishing" and regularizing might also have been done by *skemmtunarmenn* who, like the rhapsodes of Homeric tradition, memorially transmitted an originally flexible but increasingly fixed text. Finally, Taylor states that some stanzas exhibiting the least amount of formulaic repetition are those very stanzas that editors have often suspected as being literary interpolations (e.g. *Völundarkviða* 9, 14, 27 and 37; see 91–92).

Taylor also makes the first attempt at isolating formulaic themes in Eddic poetry, providing charts for a "theme of speech introduction" (50–51), and various themes describing "the hero on the battlefield" (59–62). Many of the formulas in Taylor's thematic charts appear across a wide spectrum of poems, which should caution against assuming textual borrowing on the basis of a few shared formulas (see further below). In the case of the two Atli poems, for example, Taylor observes that *Atlamál* differs in that it exhibits "an exceptionally low proportion of formulas" (63). Interestingly enough, however, a few formulas and systems cluster within groups of poems that might otherwise be suspected as products of one author, or at least one particularly cohesive tradition. For instance, the Helgi poems attest exclusively the use of the formulas for battle "fell í morgum," "örnu glaða," and "gunni at heyja."[13]

Taylor's discussion in his fourth chapter became the basis for his article published in 1963 in *Neophilologus* which, together with Sveinsson's comments and the Lehmann article discussed below, represents the first of the published applications of oral-formulaic theory to Eddic verse. Unfortunately, Taylor does not document the formulaic nature of the poems or discuss the special nature of the Eddic corpus and its transmission, as he had done in his dissertation. Instead he treats the applicability of Lord's formulations as a given, and then shows how repeated half-lines in *Völundarkviða* help underline a mythic, typological structure. These repeated half-lines he consistently terms "formulas," although as noted above, many of them repeat only within *Völundarkviða*, and others are comprised merely of two words, one of which recurs elsewhere in the corpus. Nonetheless, he does make a good case for the artistic use of repetition in the poem, and argues persuasively for the integral relationship of the swan-maiden prologue with the rest of the poem. He shows how this prologue is linked to the subsequent action, Níðuðr's attack, by the repetition of the line "kom þar af veiði / veðreygr skyti" ('came there from the woods the weather-wise marksman'), employed first when Völundr discovers his swan-bride is gone (st. 4), and again when he discovers Níðuðr's men have stolen his ring (st. 8). Furthermore, this ring, in its transfer from the swan-maiden to Níðuðr's daughter Böðvildr, links the two parts of the poem in an interesting play of sexual symbols, which include Völundr's sword (later stolen by Níðuðr) and his hammer.[14]

By a strange coincidence, the other early discussion of formulas in Eddic poetry, Winfred P. Lehmann's 1963 article "The Composition of Eddic Verse,"[15] also devotes a good deal of its attention to the artistic use of repetition in *Völundarkviða*. Lehmann focuses more on the parallels between the misfortunes of Völundr and Níðuðr, such as 11.3–4 "oc hann vacnaði / vilia lauss" ('and he awoke bereft of joy'), said of Völundr, and 31.1 "Vaki ec ávalt vilia lauss" ('I wake ever bereft of joy'), said by Níðuðr.[16]

Lehmann's examination of *Völundarkviða* forms part of a larger argument that does not quite cohere. He begins with a discussion of Parry and Lord, and in emulation of their work calls for a shift in attention to the artistic use of formulas. He remarks that Eddic poetry differs from Homeric epic verse "through restrictions in length, substance and form" (8) reminiscent of ballads, and yet he finds in the *Edda* none of the "excess" of repetition in the ballads. Consequently one can compare neither current oral epic nor ballad practice, but must instead look for internal evidence and contemporary descriptions in Old Icelandic literature. Both the *Snorra Edda* and *Egils saga* impart information about poetic composition, but only for skaldic verse. If skaldic verse is courtly, then one might suspect Eddic verse is "folk poetry." Lehmann then tests the "degree of sophistication" in *Lokasenna*, outlining a numeric structure with rune-magical overtones (10), and in *Völundarkviða*, citing the artistically employed repetitions mentioned above. He concludes that such features in the poems "may demonstrate that the Eddic poems were careful compositions by highly trained poets—not rustic products of peasant conviviality," and that Eddic poets "were not unskilled in the composition of verse and that they manipulated inherited features of form for their poetic ends" (14). One assumes he is combatting an unspoken prejudice against folk poets as "unwashed illiterates"; his unease in this regard recalls Sveinsson's. His distinction between formulas that are "aimlessly introduced" versus "carefully used for artistic effect" (14) likewise seems based on a false polarity; in what tradition would one find formulas "aimlessly introduced?" In any case, Lehmann's article, like Taylor's, did not establish the formulaic nature of Eddic poetry convincingly enough to generate much enthusiasm among contemporary critics.

Robert Kellogg first published some of his remarks on oral-formulaic theory in 1965, in an article entitled "The South Germanic Oral Tradition." Unlike his dissertation, however, his article focuses not on the *Edda* but on formulaic parallels between *Beowulf* and the Old Saxon *Heliand*, such as Sievers had pointed out a century before. Only at the very end of his article does Kellogg cite some poetic compounds shared by *Beowulf* and the *Edda*, concluding that "our knowledge of the formulas—and even more importantly, the formulaic systems—of Anglo-Saxon poetry depends upon a knowledge of the formulas and formulaic systems of *Edda, Heliand, Muspilli* and *Hildebrand*" (73).

Kellogg discusses the *Edda* at greater length in what must be, after *The Singer of Tales*, one of the most widely read discussions of oral-formulaic theory, the second chapter of his and Robert Scholes's *The Nature of Narrative* (published in 1966). This chapter presents Parry's work on Homer, and then somewhat uncritically (or else polemically) includes *Beowulf*, the *Edda*, and the *Chanson de Roland* as other representatives of oral-formulaic tradition. Kellogg's most influential contribution here, as it turned out, was in his application of the theory to *prose* composition in the sagas, arguing that the "remarkably uniform and formulaic" style of the sagas and the "parallel passages that many critics cite as examples of literary borrowing by one saga author from another are more easily explained as elements common to an oral tradition."[17]

Kellogg does, however, make a few remarks of particular relevance to Eddic composition, including the observation that "If an orally composed poem such as the Old Icelandic *Völuspá* is obscure, the difficulty must be attributed to either an inferior performance or, what is more likely, to corruption in the process of manuscript transmission" (23). That is, since he assumes that the poet is creating the text anew, Kellogg discounts the idea of garbled oral transmission of an imperfectly understood ancient text. With regard to the question of memorial transmission, he remarks that "the transcription of genuine oral performances will combine with the oral recitation of the resulting written texts to develop gradually into a quasi-literary tradition" (31).[18] Finally, he excepts the ballad, to which Eddic poems have often been compared, as a genre that has been "sufficiently influenced by the idea of a written literature and by the conception of a fixed text that individual narratives are not actually composed anew with each performance" (56).

LÖNNROTH AND THE SEVENTIES

Lars Lönnroth's 1971 article in *Speculum* criticizes Kellogg's discussion on several points. He states that the claim of improvisational composition ignores the usual assumption that Eddic poems are "from a formal point of view, closer to the ballad than to the epic, and their extreme terseness of style seems to indicate careful artistic planning rather than improvisation" (2). He claims that formulas "do not seem to play the same decisive role" in Eddic poetry, that they function rather like ballad refrains in a way that makes "a very conscious, deliberate, and artistic impression [as] well documented in the articles by Lehmann and Taylor" (2). One might again object to the implication that "oral-formulaic" in some way precludes "artistic," and Lönnroth (as he notes) is in sympathy with Sveinsson and Lehmann in this regard.

Lönnroth next considers the possibility of memorial transmission of fixed texts within the Eddic tradition. He argues, as Jabbour had done for Old English,[19] that the presence of nearly identical variant texts implies a dependence on "a more or less fixed, memorized text" (3). Against the argument that such fixity results from the influence of written recordings, he states that Saxo Grammaticus seems to have known some Eddic texts in almost the same form. Since, however, Saxo writes at about the same time as the presumed transcription of the *Edda*, and since we cannot compare his Latin translations in sufficient detail, this particular counterargument does not seem very convincing. Furthermore, Lönnroth makes clear later on in his article that some variant versions, while related closely enough to indicate a predominantly memorial transmission, also exhibit a degree of independent, formulaic composition.

Lönnroth advocates a model of performance different from the improvisatory model of *The Singer of Tales*. On the basis of *Norna-Gests þáttr*, the "sagaskemmtun" passage in *Sturlunga saga*, and the genre of *fornaldarsögur* as a whole, Lönnroth forms the hypothesis that Eddic poetry was characteristically performed as part of a *prosimetrum*. Historically, prose "had gradually taken over more and more of the narrative function from the earlier heroic lays, so that eventually only some especially dramatic speeches were highlighted in verse form" (6). Furthermore, he argues that the moments chosen for poetic treatment were characteristically those which encouraged audience identification (that is, which exemplified what he will later call the "double scene").

Since, as Taylor had argued, the *Codex Regius* as well as the *fornaldarsögur* were transcribed well after the period of active Eddic composition, one might prefer to derive some Eddic features from what Kellogg terms a "quasi-literary" period. Lönnroth does in fact suppose that Eddic poetry may have been improvised "at an early stage of the tradition" (9), and that some of the putatively older, more narrative poems reflect an earlier phase of the development towards *prosimetra*. Lönnroth realizes the difficulty of tracing this development, however, and leaves critics to resolve for themselves the degree to which the surviving texts reflect an improvisatory past.

In some respects Lönnroth's article may be seen as a careful, well-reasoned vindication of the more impressionistic observations of Heusler and Sveinsson, to the effect that in the *Edda* as against other Germanic poems, formulas "serve as ornaments and as poetic padding rather than the basic building blocks of composition" (Lönnroth, 2). Like Sveinsson also, he argues from the early formulations of oral-formulaic theory, and is not sufficiently aware of subsequent revisions by Anglo-Saxon scholars, who have also seen evidence of formulaic padding (especially in the translated verse) and memorial transmission. From his later works, it is evident that Lönnroth is committed to exploring the uses of oral-formulaic theory. But in evoking his more dismissive forbears, Lönnroth may not have sufficiently challenged the prevailing indifference of Eddic critics towards oral-formulaic theory, of which he has since had cause to complain.[20]

Lönnroth follows up on his interest in oral performance in a book-length study, *Den dubbla scenen* (published in 1978).[21] Before discussing Lönnroth's further contributions to oral-formulaic theory, however, some words about the critical assumptions underlying his book may be in order. In a 1981 article ("The New Critics of 1968"), Lönnroth described the intellectual climate in Scandinavian universities as resulting from a Kuhnian revolution in scholarly assumptions. After the student revolutions of 1968, a group of Marxist-inspired *ideologikritiker* played an important role in this new emphasis, which also involved a synthesis of semiotics, psychoanalysis, and German *Geistegeschichte*. The academically established members of this group then took part in research collectives, including a new *History of Danish Literature*. Lönnroth was participating in the writing of the medieval volume;[22] he describes its overall program as involving socioeconomic and semiotic analyses of the period, as well as close readings of representative texts. More specifically, the authors hoped to describe an ideological shift from a pagan society based on ties of kinship, to a Christian society based on ties of feudal obligation. As an example of close reading, Lönnroth compares the heroic *Bjarkamál* with Saxo's Latin translation of it, and discusses the influence upon the latter of classical aesthetics, clerical morality, and ideas of feudal order.

Lönnroth's chapter on *Völuspá* in *Den dubbla scenen* provides an analysis similar to those of the *ideologikritiker* in its focus on the reception of the poem by its thirteenth-century audience, and in its attempts to determine the performance context and ideological function of the poem. In addition, Lönnroth's chapter may be seen as a direct response to Sigurður Nordal's classic study of *Völuspá*. Nordal had created a picture of a tormented poet undergoing a crisis of faith amidst the volcanic landscapes of millennial Iceland. Against this view Lönnroth offers a prophetic persona through which the dominant ideology (of the powerful chieftains and their clerical allies) authenticates itself in myth.

In the first part of his study, Lönnroth presents his earlier speculations about Eddic poetry as something of an established fact. He outlines the development of Germanic heroic poetry from improvised, formulaic compositions to the stanzaic, dramatic, less formulaic, and memorially transmitted poems of the *Edda*. This model of development leads him to maintain that in Eddic poetry "there was no longer a great need for ready-made formulas" (33).

Nonetheless, Lönnroth does find it convenient to invoke formulaic pressures and alliterative demands in a few instances. He writes, "that we now speak of Ginnungagap as a name for the Chaos of Old Norse mythology may be due to the purely accidental circumstance that a poet or reciter needed to fill out the verse line with a word beginning with *g*" (44). Similarly, he suggests that alliterative demands and a formulaic parallel motivate the choice of "sunnan" and "hægri" in "Sól varp *s*unnan" ('The sun cast from the south') and "hendi inni *h*ægri" ('[her] right hand,' st. 5). He also sees as formulaic the opening line "Ár var alda," 'in times of yore,' traditionally employed to invoke a distant *ur*-time. One does in fact find the identical half-line used to begin the poem *Helgakviða Hundingsbana I*, although here the reference is to a less distant heroic past. Presumably Lönnroth was also reminded of the second half-line of *Beowulf,* "in geardagum."

Elsewhere Lönnroth calls the line "Þá gengo regin öll / á röcstóla" ('Then all the gods went to their judgment-seats') a "ceremonial formula," repeated three times in *Völuspá*, "each time in a connection that emphasizes the holiness and indispensability of the legislative assembly" (46). Since this line acts as a refrain in *Völuspá*, one may wish to be more circumspect in terming it a formula although similar expressions occur in *Þrymskviða* 14 and *Baldrs draumar* 1:

> Senn vóro æsir allir á þingi,
> ok ásynior allar á máli
> ok um þat réðo ríkir tívar
> [Then the gods all assembled, and the goddesses all conversed and the mighty powers deliberated].

Lönnroth concludes with a rather puzzling reference to oral-formulaic theory; he writes:

> Passages that have been regarded by other commentators as obscure survivals of an older *ur*-text . . . can more naturally be explained on

the basis of Parry and Lord's formulaic theory and on the interplay
between the reciter/sybil and a thirteenth-century Icelandic audience
. . . Why complicate matters by postulating a several hundred year-
old oral textual tradition which in any case can never be verified?
(51)

This statement appears to represent a shift in emphasis from his earlier
claims about memorial transmission. Primarily he is seeking a justification
for interpreting the poem in light of thirteenth-century ideological
considerations; but in so doing he seems also to suggest a formulaic poet
who recreates the text in response to a particular audience. In a subsequent
(1982) article on the collocation "iörð/upphiminn" in creation myth
contexts,[23] Lönnroth admits that "an oral performance will always contain
an *element* of improvisation" (311), and considers that the different
formulas employed in the variant versions of *Völuspá* as "left-overs from
. . . an earlier, more 'fluid' stage in the oral tradition" (312).

If he has indeed moved closer to a Parryite view of oral
(re-)composition, then Lönnroth may have been influenced by statements
made in Preben Meulengracht Sørensen's *Saga og samfund* (published in
Danish in 1977; in English translation, 1993). Like Lönnroth, Sørensen
emphasizes the contemporary reception of a text, and may therefore have
been attracted to a view of transmission that emphasizes continual
updating rather than conservative preservation. In any case, Sørensen
provides a number of arguments against strictly memorial transmission, in
conjunction with a discussion of methods of dating texts. He finds it
improbable that a poet would remember and recite "poems whose form
and speech were authentic to the period two or three hundred years
earlier" (83), while at the same time composing new poems in a
contemporary language. He considers it more reasonable to assume a
poetic language that incorporated archaic elements, to be used particularly
when a more ceremonial tone was desired. He admits that the evidence
from variant versions of *Völuspá* does suggest that the text was
comparatively fixed in the thirteenth century. As Taylor had done before
him, however, Sørensen emphasizes that parts of the tradition were at that
time no longer living, a situation that resulted, for instance, in the
imperfect preservation of *Hamðismál*. The poems preserved in the *Codex*

Regius, with its preference for terse, dramatic versions, were recorded primarily from performances by trained skalds, that is, poets who, like Snorri, had a taste for the economies of skaldic verse; Sørensen even suggests that the *Codex Regius* may have been intended as an anthology to accompany Snorri's 'textbook' (80). A few of the poems, such as *Atlamál*, suggest a more sprawling, popular verse and there are enough incidental references in the sagas to suggest the existence of other popular forms which, however, were largely ignored by the transcribers of official culture. The allusiveness of the poems also suggests an unpreserved background of more expansive versions.

To a certain extent Sørensen, like Kellogg before him, applies oral-formulaic theory broadly and polemically to the Icelandic situation. His contention that an oral culture seeks to preserve content rather than form seems oversimplified, especially if such content resides partly in formulas that already have a formal representation. I sympathize with his skepticism about attempts at dating the poems, although he does not deal with apparent quotes from Eddic poems in skaldic verse.[24] He maintains that Eddic poetry is less formulaic than Serbo-Croatian poetry, and yet sees fit to derive "general laws" (76) from the Serbo-Croatian application. As we have seen, however, by the end of his discussion, Sørensen offers some interesting scenarios for the period of Eddic transcription.

In an article, "Eddic Poetry as Oral Poetry," which appeared in 1983 (but which had been written in 1974), Joseph Harris offers a noteworthy evaluation of the *Edda* as oral poetry. He first presents a typological scheme for oral traditions, based on a polarity of improvised versus deliberative composition, and of improvised versus memorial transmission. Harris allows for a wide variety of combinations along these axes; his scheme represents a significant improvement over the earlier "oral versus written" dichotomy. To his scheme I would add *dictation*; many medieval authors dictated their compositions to scribes (who wrote on wax tablets, at least in the early period) and this writing technology must also have had its effects.[25] In addition to technology, however, the *models* that authors had in mind must have played an important role. Many sorts of texts may have been composed deliberatively and 'orally,' i.e., in one's head; a distinguishing factor will be whether those texts were composed after an apprenticeship to oral-traditional performances or to literary models from the manuscript culture.

According to Harris, Lönnroth's model had distinguished between only "a tradition with deliberative composition (which is not especially formulaic) and memorial transmission which is occasionally botched by improvisation (indicated by formulas)." In contrast, Harris suggests "the possibility of variations being those of 'conscious revisers,' albeit impeccably *oral* revisers" (213). He then examines the parallel *sennur* (or abusive exchanges) in *Helgakviða Hundingsbana I* and *II* (HHu I and II), and concludes that both poets composed orally from a remembered *Völsungakviða in forna*, but that the poet of HHu I was a "skaldic reviser." Recall that Sørensen, too, hypothesizes that skaldic poets shaped the versions of Eddic poems that were transcribed into the *Codex Regius*. But in suggesting a deliberative, oral reviser, Harris makes an important contribution to the issue of textual borrowing in oral poetry. He notes that "Eddic scholarship seems to have overestimated the individual borrowings and undervalued the force of collective tradition, especially at the level of lexical choice and phrasing." And yet with the Helgi poems, and perhaps also some Old English poems (such as *Daniel* and *Azarias*), "it is impossible to overlook some kind of genetic relationship" (224).

The Helgi poems, according to Harris, also provide evidence for additional scribal revision by the redactor of the *Codex Regius*. This redactor, seeking to present two complementary treatments of the Helgi legend, summarizes in prose those parts of HHu II that he apparently considers "identical" with HHu I. At the appropriate point in HHu II the redactor cites one stanza of the shared *senna*, with a reference back to HHu I. A few stanzas later, however, he abruptly reintroduces this passage, having "noticed too late that the flyting was different" (216). When he reached the last two stanzas, and apparently "progressively realized that [these] stanzas were identical," he began to abbreviate heavily. For the line "satt at mæla" 'to speak the truth' in HHu I 46:4, for instance, he merely writes "s.a.m." (HHu II 24:4). Harris's close attention to such manuscript details yields important new insights for understanding the scribe's role in transmitting formulaic verse.

A few other critics writing in the 1970's addressed brief remarks to oral-formulaic theory and Eddic poetry. In a 1974 article, John Stephens shows how the poet of *Atlakviða* manipulates traditional and innovative forms to "suggest certain attitudes toward his material" (56). For example, Stephens notes that both Gunnarr and Högni's deaths invoke the gnomic observation, "svá scal frǽcna" ('so shall a brave man do'). In making this parallel, Stephens suggests, the poet values equally two kinds of heroism: "the courage to fight against tremendous odds, and the courage to die with a quiet defiance, lips sealed" (60). Stephens's article thus resembles those of Taylor and Lehmann in its demonstration of the artful use of formulaic diction.

In a 1976 article, Edward R. Haymes opposes Heusler's *Liedertheorie*, which "chose the lays of the Elder Edda as the typical model for the Germanic *Heldenlied*" (46). As Hans Kuhn had argued, however, the allusiveness of Eddic poems suggests that they are derivative rather than primary versions. Haymes, unlike Kuhn and perhaps also Lönnroth, argues that these hypothetical early versions were not prose narratives but rather improvised, oral-formulaic compositions exhibiting the epic breadth of *Beowulf* and *Hildebrandslied*. The Eddic poems, on the other hand, represent a later, predominantly memorial tradition; they may well have been composed, as Einarsson had suggested (21), "in (Norway or) Iceland by a group of poets related in culture and vying with one another in treating topics and characters each from his own point of view."

While awaiting the appearance of his article on the *Edda* as oral poetry (discussed above), Joseph Harris presented a few related observations in "The *senna*: from description to literary theory" (1979). He advocates building upon such native genres, rather than procrustean schema taken over from Lord's South Slavic model (in *The Singer of Tales*). Harris then relates the *senna* to comparable speech-events discussed in folklore and anthropological studies.

Anatoly Liberman, writing in 1978, considers that Magoun's pupils "failed to prove their point (sc. of an oral "Beowulf")" (442), but nonetheless credits Parry with showing "what formulas were meant for and how they originally came into being" (443). Drawing on Eric Havelock's *Preface to Plato*, Liberman then argues that skaldic poetry represents a shift from the "formulaic mind" to "a more individualized way of thinking" (444) that involved a more unmediated relation to current events and a conception of individual authorship. In his discussion Liberman occasionally takes issue with M.I. Steblin-Kamenskij, a Russian scholar who had discussed oral-formulaic theory in connection with conceptions of authorship among saga-writers.

THE EIGHTIES

A collection of essays on Old Norse literature edited in 1986 by John Lindow, *et al.*, includes two articles relating to oral composition, each translated from Russian. References to the latter of these articles, by Elena Gurevic, have been incorporated into my first chapter, and will not be repeated here. The other article is by Eleazar M. Meletinsky, and first appeared in Russian in 1978. Its subject is "commonplaces" in Eddic poetry, including epithets, repetitions and "ritual" actions and situations. While the article frequently mentions "formulas," these are not defined or clearly related to Parryite discussions of oral-formulaic theory. Hence, while it is interesting to note that in *Völuspá* "*ár* defines the ancient epoch when order was created out of chaos, and *unz* points to the beginning of the reverse process" (17), it is not clear just what "*ár* and *unz* formulas" are; Meletinksy later calls these words the "kernel of the commonplace" (22). His final discussion of parallelisms, epic variation and echoing in the Edda, Russian *byliny* and Karelo-Finnish "runes" (28) is even more vague, since no examples are cited. Apparently some of this material is treated in greater detail in his *"Edda" i rannie formi èposa* (Moscow, 1968).[26]

A number of the published papers from the 1988 Saga Conference (published in 1990) address or touch upon oral-formulaic theory and Eddic poetry. In an article entitled "The Prehistory of Eddic Poetry,"[27] Robert Kellogg first makes some general comments about "the consequences for *Edda* scholarship of the Parry-Lord hypothesis" (187). Eddic poems would exist "as texts only at the moment of performance" (188); between performances there would only be an abstract "competence." The performer would speak for tradition, would not invent a separate narrator, and there would be a greater immediacy between audience and performer. Formulaic elements in the *Edda* are best seen as "traces of the compositional habits of performers who composed orally" (190), by which Kellogg means improvisation in performance; he rejects the idea of "a minstrel who recites a text fixed in his memory" (189; and see 196).

Kellogg then turns to the question of Germanic epic. Oral epic, "an especially rich cultural competence" (192), can be textualized only if writing technology is introduced in such a way that "the older, aristocratic epic synthesis does not collapse" (193); but "Germanic society, under the influence of invasions, migrations and classical models, evolved away from the aristocratic-heroic type faster than had the archaic Greek" (194). While the formal aspects that distinguished oral poetry continued, the "epic impulse" by the thirteenth century diffused into various kinds of sagas and Eddic poetry, which concisely treated aspects of the gods, wisdom attributed to them, and a cycle of heroic episodes (196). This view of Germanic literary history reverses the Heuslerian idea that Eddic-type poems evolved into epic (cp. also Haymes above). In the *Codex Regius*, the literate Collector dissociates himself from the epic materials of antiquity. He comments on and organizes the material, referring to poems by fixed titles, thereby indicating that for him the traditional plots have become "discrete eddic-sized units" (198), that is, literary texts.

Kellogg's paper adheres closely to the Parry-Lord model for some aspects, such as improvisation in performance, which more revisionist writers like Harris have challenged. At the opposite pole, the Saga Conference paper by Jónas Kristjánsson, "Stages in the Composition of Eddic Poetry," takes a few potshots at oral-formulaic theory of a sort not seen since the earliest objections by Sveinsson. Kristjánsson sneers at the "theory that has been very fashionable in recent years, according to which the Eddic poems are considered comparable to Serbo-Croatian folk-poems or songs." The "American scholars" Parry and Lord "studied these poems—if that is the right word for them" (202; Jónas does not mention that Parry began studying Homeric verse; presumably that comparison would not have been so self-evidently ludicrous). "Some people" thus claim Eddic poems "are of the same kind as the Serbo-Croat songs, that is that they did not have any fixed form until they were written down" (202). Lönnroth is quoted approvingly for his "entirely negative" conclusions (203), namely that Eddic poems were carefully and 'artistically' planned and memorized rather than improvised. We are told to consider *Völuspá*: "Even if it contains one or two turns of phrase that are found elsewhere" (compare Sveinsson's demotion of formulas), it was not improvised. "It is obvious that this poem was from the beginning carefully thought out in content and polished in form" (203). Kristjánsson then quotes a stanza that has "enough pure poetry to move our souls deeply," which apparently no oral or oral-derived poem could do. For the rest of his paper, Kristjánsson considers a more classic (and not merely fashionable) question, the dating of Eddic poetry.

Kristjánsson's remarks would make more sense if directed, like Sveinsson's, at the earliest versions of oral-formulaic theory. As John Miles Foley has recently suggested, many early opponents of the theory did so not so much as "a refusal to acknowledge oral roots but rather a defense against the abrogation of aesthetics that such an acknowledgment seemed to demand" ("Orality," 35). Kristjánsson similarly rejects oral-formulaic theory on aesthetic (as well as nationalistic) grounds; improvisational composition yields bad Serbo-Croatian poetry, not soul-stirring Icelandic poetry.[28] But improvisation is no longer the only model proposed for formulaic poetry. Composition in formulas may likewise seem less aesthetically objectionable if considered as, again in Foley's words, "much less a matter of manipulating a Lego-set collection of substitutable parts than of learning to speak an idiom that is the issue of traditional rules and processes operating on phraseology and thematic structure" (41).

In his Saga Conference paper, "On the Classification of Eddic Poetry in View of the Oral Theory," Gísli Sigurðsson maintains that the orality of Eddic poetry cannot be proved or disproved, but that it is "more fruitful" (246) to assume that Lord's model does apply. Despite complications arising from the written transmission of Eddic poems, they must have had a prior existence in oral tradition. With paired Eddic treatments like *Atlakviða* and *Atlamál*, one need not be more ancient than the other (as in the opinion of Kristjánsson) but rather intended for a different kind of audience. The skaldic diction of heroic emphasis in the former poem may imply a courtly audience; the everyday language and domestic focus of the latter may imply an audience of Icelandic farmers. In addition to different classes, the poems may have favored different genders as well. The latter poem introduces the wives of the heroes Gunnar and Högni as well as details about the domestic activities of women.

While Sigurðsson's demarcation along these gender lines may be a bit too clear-cut—surely men can be interested in the activities of women and vice versa—his emphasis on audience disrupts certain traditional philological assumptions in the way that recent theories of (inter)textuality have been challenging older methods of literary history and source criticism.[29] Sigurðsson specifically questions the method of critics like Theodore Andersson who treat the Nibelung legend "as a unity" and the relevant Eddic poems as "pieces in a jigsaw puzzle" (252). Apparent inconsistencies in, for instance, the motivation of Guðrún result from the ill-advised attempt to force the "female-orientated poems" into "a general frame-work of the heroic poems" (255). Sigurðsson is a young critic trained in Iceland and Dublin, and clearly enjoys taking on the established views of critics like Andersson and Kristjánsson.

In her Saga Conference paper, "*Völuspá* and the Composition of Eddic Verse," Judy Quinn examines the differences between the two extant manuscript versions of the poem, texts that are "a consequence of divergent oral traditions" (303). Rather than conflating the two texts into one reconstructed putatively authorial version, she examines each version on its own terms, then characterizes the main areas of divergence. As she notes in her 1994 survey, "*Völuspá* in Twentieth-Century Scholarship in English," her approach (and that of other scholars incorporating insights from oral theory) is in sympathy with the post-structuralist "radical critique of [the] notion of authorship" (130).

THE NINETIES

In other studies Quinn has continued to explore the interface of oral and literary environments. In "The Naming of Eddic Mythological Poems in Medieval Manuscripts" (1990), Quinn provides a useful table of the various names given by scribes and modern editors to poems in the *Codex Regius*, related Eddic manuscripts, and in the *Snorra Edda*. She argues that in the oral-traditional environment, names for poems were usually composed of a main actor (e.g. Loki) and a speech act or genre (e.g. *Lokasenna*, 'Loki's flyting'). These names could refer to a range of oral treatments of the same subject. In compiling different versions for written manuscripts, however, scribes differentiated among versions by adding characterizations such as 'the shorter' or 'the Greenlandic' (e.g. *Sigurðarkviða in skamma; Atlamál in grænlensku*).

In "Verseform and voice in eddic poems: the discourses of *Fáfnismál*," Quinn examines the use in Eddic poetry of two meters, *ljóðaháttr* and *fornyrðislag*, arguing that "the discursive style appropriate to particular verbal exchanges depended in part on the nature of the speech-act . . . and in part on the identities of the speakers" (101). After surveying metrical use in several poems, she focuses on the "poetic finesse" (120) of metrical shifts in *Fáfnismál*. Her study is representative of a more broadly-based oral theory that incorporates related approaches such as speech-act theory and discourse analysis.

In conclusion, we may observe that for Eddic poetry, oral-formulaic theory has made a fitful progress; it has been asserted and re-introduced a number of times and has had to compete against a unsympathetic body of received opinion (especially Heusler's negative evaluation of the role of formulas). In consequence, much basic statistical research has never been attempted; Eddic criticism lacks reference works long ago provided for *Beowulf* criticism such as Lynch on alliterative collocations or Watts on repeated half-lines. The contributions by Lönnroth, Sørensen, Harris, and Quinn may indicate, however, that oral-formulaic theory has made a foothold among Scandinavianists. Furthermore, their creative re-interpretation of the various factors involved in the composition and transmission of formulaic verse should serve as an inspiration for oral-formulaists working in other literatures.

NOTES

1. In 1985, Harris published a bibliographical essay on Eddic poetry, including a section on 'Eddic Poetry as Oral Poetry.' Our works are complementary to the extent that he has not summarized the critical literature (through 1983) in detail, although his brief characterizations are always incisive. His essay should also be consulted for related topics such as the performance of Eddic poetry. John Miles Foley's *Oral-Formulaic Theory and Research: An Introduction and Annotated Bibliography* (1985) provides brief summaries of a few of the works discussed here, as well as items dealing principally with skaldic poetry or Old Icelandic prose.

2. So also Andersson ("Oral-Formulaic"), following Heusler but incorporating some arguments from Harris and Lönnroth, discussed below.

3. Cp. Griffith: "It is the poet's rhetoric that is the proper study of formulaic analysis" (196).

4. For a detailed summary of "book-prose" versus "free-prose" approaches, see Andersson, *Problem*.

5. See also Harris, "Eddic Poetry," 120.

6. All translations from German are mine.

7. Recently, however, a number of critics have been proposing different models for the meeting of oral and written influences in Old English poetic composition. See Opland; Russom, "Verse"; Foley, *Theory*; Fry, "The Memory of Caedmon"; and O'Keeffe, *Visible Song*, as well as the writings of Taylor, Lönnroth, and Harris discussed below.

8. For a definition of this term, see Chapter One.

9. Pages 148–50 and 162 in his *Íslenzkar bókmenntir í fornöld* (printed in 1962), which I will quote in translation.

10. See Andersson, *Problem*.

11. Kellogg published a version of this concordance, with different introductory matter, in 1988.

12. Here he exaggerates, for just as in Old English, some texts do exhibit variants in alliterating position, suggesting authorial rather than scribal variation; see the discussion of Lönnroth below.

13. The latter two formulas, however, appear in nearly identical passages; see the comments by Harris, discussed below.

14. Taylor writes that the "emasculated" Völundr "makes himself a hammer" (231). Most translators, however, interpret that Völundr was hamstrung, not castrated, and that he does not forge a hammer, but rather *with* a hammer ("sló hamri," st. 20).

15. In a footnote (12), Lehmann states that he first delivered his paper at the Modern Language Association Convention in 1961, after which Paul Taylor informed him of his own work on the subject. Lehmann then cites Taylor's article, which had just appeared.

16. The phrase "vilia lauss," incidentally, recalls a number of similar expressions employed in the Old English elegies (see Greenfield). One of these elegies (*Deor*) recounts the misfortunes of Weland and Beaduhild (Völundr and Böðvildr).

17. As noted in the previous chapter, oral-formulaists had advanced a similar explanation for the occurrence in Old English poetry of *Parallelstellen*, which hitherto had been cited as evidence of common authorship.

18. For Old English, Kellogg notes King Alfred's "modern" attitude toward literacy (*Nature*, 37). Recalling that Alfred memorized "Saxon" poems from a book, and that he instigated the transcription of vernacular poems, one might also suspect that some features of the extant Old English poetic texts reflect a similar quasi-literary tradition; see also Fry's remarks on Alfred in "The Memory of Caedmon."

19. Page 3. Lönnroth mentions in a footnote (9) that he had come upon Jabbour's article after completing his own.

20. See his 1970 review of Ursula Dronke's *The Poetic Edda*, as well as the chapter from *Den dubbla scenen* discussed below.

21. My translation of Lönnroth's chapter on *Völuspá* will appear in a volume of essays on the *Edda* edited by Carolyne Larrington and myself for Garland Publishing. Material from this chapter will be cited in translation but with page references to the Swedish edition.

22. This volume appeared in 1987; see the review by Jesch.

23. Hieatt, following Lönnroth, isolates a "theme of creation" in Germanic verse.

24. See Einarsson, 22 and Kristjánsson, *Eddas*, 29.

25. See Brown, 49.

26. Meletinsky mentions (16) an English edition, *The Elder Edda and Early Forms of Epic Poetry* (Frankfurt, 1987), but I have not been able to track down any such translation.

27. Kellogg ("Literacy," 1991) is essentially a reworking of this paper, covering much the same ground, but in slightly different proportions.

28. Kristjánsson's 1988 survey, *Eddas and Sagas* (translated into English in 1992), makes several references to oral transmission of Eddic poetry (e.g. 47–49), without reference to oral-formulaic theory.

29. See Lees, and Clayton & Rothstein.

Bibliography

Acker, Paul. "*Alvíssmál.*" *Medieval Scandinavia: An Encyclopedia.* Eds. Phillip Pulsiano, *et al.* New York: Garland, 1993. 11–12.

————. "Dwarf-Lore in *Alvíssmál.*" *Mythological Poems of the Elder Edda: A Case Book.* Eds. Paul Acker, and Carolyne Larrington. New York: Garland, forthcoming.

————. "The Old English *Rune Poem* and Formulaic Theory." *Language and Style* 22 (1989): 149–65.

Andersson, Theodore. "Did the Poet of *Atlamál* Know *Atlaqviða?*" In Glendinning, 243–57.

————. "The lays in the lacuna of *Codex Regius.*" *Speculum Norroenum. Norse Studies in Memory of Gabriel Turville-Petre.* Eds. Ursula Dronke, et. al. Odense: Odense UP, 1981. 6–26.

————. "Die Oral-Formulaic Poetry im Germanischen." *Heldensage und Heldendichtung im Germanischen.* Ed. Heinrich Beck. Berlin: Walter de Gruyter, 1988. 1–14.

————. *The Problem of Icelandic Saga Origins. A Historical Survey.* New Haven: Yale UP, 1964.

Barthes, Roland. "The Structuralist Activity." Trans. Richard Howard. *Contemporary Literary Criticism: Literary and Cultural Studies.* 2nd ed. Eds. Robert Con Davis, and Ronald Schleifer. New York: Longman, 1989. 170–74.

Bartlett, Adeline Courtney. *The Larger Rhetorical Patterns in Anglo-Saxon Poetry.* New York: Columbia UP, 1935.

Benson, Larry D. "The Literary Character of Anglo-Saxon Formulaic Poetry." *PMLA* 81 (1966): 334–41.

Berlin, Gail Ivy. "Memorization in Anglo-Saxon England: Some Case Studies." *Oral Tradition in the Middle Ages.* Ed. W.F.H. Nicolaisen. Binghamton: State U of New York, 1995. 97–113.

Bessinger, J.B., ed. *A Concordance to the Anglo-Saxon Poetic Records*. Ithaca: Cornell UP, 1978.

Bethurum, Dorothy, ed. *The Homilies of Wulfstan*. Oxford: Clarendon, 1957.

———. "Stylistic Features of Old English Laws." *Modern Language Review* 27 (1932): 263–79.

Bjork, Robert E., and John D. Niles, eds. *A Beowulf Handbook*. Lincoln: U of Nebraska P, 1997.

Bjork, Robert E., and Anita Obermeier. "Date, Provenance, Author, Audiences." In Bjork and Niles, 13–34.

Bonjour, Adrien. "Beowulf and the Beasts of Battle." *PMLA* 72 (1957): 563–73.

Bosworth, Joseph, and T. Northcote Toller. *An Anglo-Saxon Dictionary*. Oxford: Oxford UP, 1898; rpt. 1954. Supplement by Toller, 1921; Addenda by Alistair Campbell, 1972.

Brook, G.L., and R.F. Leslie, eds. *Layamon: Brut*. EETS os 250. London: Oxford UP, 1963.

Brown, Michelle P. *Anglo-Saxon Manuscripts*. Toronto: U of Toronto P, 1991.

Bullough, D.A. "The Educational tradition in England from Alfred to Aelfric: Teaching *Utriusque Linguae*." *Settimane di studi del centro italiano di studi sull'alto medioevo* 19 (1971): 453–94.

Cassidy, Frederic G. "How Free was the Anglo-Saxon Scop?" *Franciplegius: Medieval and Linguistic Studies in Honor of Francis Peabody Magoun, Jr*. Eds. Jess B. Bessinger, and Robert P. Creed. New York: New York UP, 1965. 75–85.

Cassidy, Frederic G., and Richard N. Ringler, eds. *Bright's Old English Grammar and Reader*. 3rd ed. New York: Holt, 1971.

Chase, Colin, ed. *The Dating of Beowulf*. Toronto: Toronto UP, 1981.

Chickering, Howell D., Jr. *Beowulf: A Dual-Language Edition*. Garden City, NY: Anchor, 1977.

Clark, Francelia Mason. *Theme and Oral Epic in Beowulf*. Milman Parry Studies in Oral Tradition. Eds. Stephen A. Mitchell, and Gregory Nagy. New York: Garland, 1995.

Clark, George. "The Traveler Recognizes His Goal: A Theme in Anglo-Saxon Poetry." *JEGP* 64 (1965): 645–59.

Clayton, Jay, and Eric Rothstein, eds. *Influence and Intertextuality in Literary History*. Madison: U of Wisconsin P, 1991.

Cleasby, Richard, and Gudbrand Vigfusson. *An Icelandic-English Dictionary*. 2nd ed. Oxford: Clarendon, 1957.

Clemoes, Peter. *Interactions of Thought and Language in Old English Poetry*. Cambridge: Cambridge UP, 1995.

―――. "King Alfred's Debt to Vernacular Poetry: the Evidence of *ellen* and *cræft*." *Words, Texts and Manuscripts: Studies in Anglo-Saxon Culture Presented to Helmut Gneuss on the Occasion of his Sixty-Fifth Birthday*. Ed. M. Korhammer. Woodbridge: Brewer, 1992.

Clunies Ross, Margaret. "The Anglo-Saxon and Norse *Rune Poems*: a comparative study." *Anglo-Saxon England* 19 (1990): 23–39.

Conner, Patrick. "Schematization of Oral-Formulaic Processes in Old English Poetry." *Language and Style* 5 (1972): 204–20.

Creed, Robert P. "Preface." *Oral Traditional Literature: A Festschrift for Albert Bates Lord*. Ed. John Miles Foley. Columbus: Slavica, 1981. 17–21.

―――. "Studies in the Technique of Composition of the Beowulf Poetry in Brit. Mus. Cotton Vitellius A.xv." Diss. Harvard U, 1955.

Crowne, David K. "The Hero on the Beach: An Example of Composition by Theme in Anglo-Saxon Poetry." *Neuphilologische Mitteilungen* 61 (1960): 362–72.

Curschmann, Michael. "Oral Poetry in Medieval English, French, and German Literature: Some Notes on Recent Research." *Speculum* 42 (1967): 36–52.

Derolez, Rene. *Runica Manuscripta*. Brugge: De Tempel, 1954.

Derrida, Jacques. "Structure, Sign, and Play in the Discourse of the Human Sciences." Trans. Richard Macksey. *Contemporary Literary Criticism: Literary and Cultural Studies*. 2nd ed. Eds. Robert Con Davis, and Ronald Schleifer. New York: Longman, 1989. 230–48.

Diamond, Robert E. "The Diction of the Signed Poems of Cynewulf." *Philological Quarterly* 38 (1959): 228–41.

Dickins, Bruce. *Runic and Heroic Poems of the Old Teutonic Peoples*. Cambridge: Cambridge UP, 1915; rpt. New York: Kraus, 1968.

Doane, A.N., and Carol Braun Pasternack, eds. *Vox intexta: Orality and Textuality in the Middle Ages*. Madison: U of Wisconsin P, 1991.

Dobbie, see Krapp.

Dronke, Ursula. *The Poetic Edda*. Vol. 1, *Heroic Poems*. Oxford: Clarendon, 1969.

Dumézil, Georges. *Gods of the Ancient Norsemen*. 1959. Ed. Einar Haugen. Trans. John Lindow, *et al*. Berkeley: U of California P, 1973.

Einarsson, Stéfan. *A History of Icelandic Literature*. New York: Johns Hopkins, 1957.

Faulkes, Anthony, ed. *Snorri Sturluson. Edda. Háttatal*. Oxford: Clarendon, 1991.

Finch, R.G. "The Treatment of Poetic Sources by the Compiler of *Völsunga Saga*." *Saga-Book of the Viking Society* 16.4 (1965): 315–53.

Fix, Hans. "Poetisches im altisländischen Recht. Zur Zwil-lingsformel in Grágás und Jónsbók." *Sprachen und Computer. Festschrift zum 75. Geburtstag von Hans Eggers 9. Juli 1982*. Ed. Hans Fix. Berlin: AQ-Verlag, 1982. 187–206.

Fjalldal, Magnús. "Kenning Lords og Parrys um tillurð og varðveizlu munnlegs kveðskapar." *Andvari* n.f. 22 (1980): 89–96.

Foley, John Miles. *Immanent Art: From Structure to Meaning in Traditional Oral Epic*. Bloomington: Indiana UP, 1991.

–––––. "Literary Art and Oral Tradition in Old English and Serbian Poetry." *Anglo-Saxon England* 12 (1983): 183–214.

–––––. *Oral-Formulaic Theory and Research. An Introduction and Annotated Bibliography*. New York: Garland, 1985.

–––––. "Orality, Textuality, and Interpretation." In Doane and Pasternack, 34–45.

–––––. "Texts that Speak to Readers Who Hear: Old English Poetry and the Languages of Oral Tradition." In Frantzen, 1991, 141–56.

–––––. *The Theory of Oral Composition: History and Methodology*. Bloomington: Indiana UP, 1988.

–––––. *Traditional Oral Epic: The Odyssey, Beowulf and the Serbo-Croatian Return Song*. Berkeley: U of California P, 1990.

Frantzen, Allen J., ed. *Speaking Two Languages: Traditional Disciplines and Contemporary Theory in Medieval Studies*. Albany: State U of New York P, 1991.

Frazer, James George. *The Golden Bough: A Study in Magic and Religion.* 3rd ed. New York: Macmillan, 1935.

Fry, Donald K., Jr. "The Hero on the Beach in *Finnsburg.*" *Neuphilologische Mitteilungen* 67 (1966): 27–31.

———. "The Heroine on the Beach in *Judith.*" *Neuphilologische Mitteilungen* 68 (1967): 168–84.

———. "The Memory of Caedmon." *Oral Traditional Literature. A Festschrift for Albert Bates Lord.* Ed. John Miles Foley. Columbus: Slavica, 1981. 282–93.

———. "Old English Formulaic Themes and Type-Scenes." *Neophilologus* 52 (1968): 48–53.

———. "Old English Formulas and Systems." *English Studies* 48 (1967): 193–204.

———. "Two Voices in *Widsith.*" *Mediaevalia* 6 (1980): 37–56.

———. "Variation and Economy in *Beowulf.*" *Modern Philology* 65 (1968): 353–56.

Glendinning, Robert J., and Haraldur Bessason, eds. *Edda: A Collection of Essays.* Manitoba: U of Manitoba P, 1983.

Gordon, E.V. *An Introduction to Old Norse.* 2nd ed. rev. A.R. Taylor. Oxford: Oxford UP, 1957; rpt. 1962.

Greenfield, Stanley B. "The Formulaic Expression of the Theme of Exile in Anglo-Saxon Poetry." *Speculum* 30 (1955): 200–06.

Griffith, M.S. "Convention and originality in the Old English 'beasts of battle' typescene." *Anglo-Saxon England* 22 (1993): 179–99.

Güntert, Hermann. *Von der Sprache der Götter und Geister: Bedeutungsgeschichtliche Untersuchungen zur homerischen und eddischen Göttersprache.* Halle: M. Niemeyer, 1921.

Gurevic, Elena A. "The formulaic pair in Eddic poetry." In Lindow, 32–55.

Hainsworth, J.B. *The Flexibility of the Homeric Formula.* Oxford: Oxford UP, 1968.

Hall, J.R. "Perspective and Wordplay in the Old English *Rune Poem.*" *Neophilologus* 61 (1977): 453–60.

Halsall, Maureen. *The Old English Rune Poem: a critical edition.* Toronto: U of Toronto P, 1981.

Halvorsen, E.F. Untitled review of Dronke in *Review of English Studies* N.S. 22 (1971): 319–22.

Hamel, Mary, ed. *Morte Arthure: A Critical Edition.* Garland Medieval Texts, 9. Gen. ed. A.S.G. Edwards. New York: Garland, 1984.

Harris, Joseph. "Eddic Poetry." *Old Norse-Icelandic Poetry: A Critical Guide.* Eds. Carol J. Clover, and John Lindow. Islandica, 45. Ithaca: Cornell UP, 1985. 68–156.

———. "Eddic Poetry as Oral Poetry: The Evidence of Parallel Passages in the Helgi Poems for Questions of Composition and Performance." In Glendinning, 210–42.

———. "A Nativist Approach to *Beowulf:* The Case of Germanic Elegy." *Companion to Old English Poetry.* Eds. Henk Aertsen, and Rolf H. Bremmer. Amsterdam: VU UP, 1994. 45–62.

———. "Reflections on Genre and Intertextuality in Eddic Poetry (with Special Reference to *Grottasöngr*)." In *Poetry,* 231–43.

———. ""The *senna:* from description to literary theory." *Michigan Germanic Studies* 5.1 (1979): 65–74.

Hartmann, R.R.K., and F.C. Stork. *Dictionary of Language and Linguistics.* New York: Wiley, 1972.

Havelock, Eric. *Preface to Plato.* Cambridge: Harvard UP, 1963.

Haymes, Edward R. "Oral poetry and the Germanic *Heldenlied.*" *Rice University Studies* 62.2 (1976): 47–54.

Hermansson, Halldór. *Catalogue of Runic Literature.* London: Oxford UP, 1918.

Heusler, Andreas. *Die altgermanische Dichtung.* Berlin-Neubabelsberg: Athenaion, 1923.

Heusler, Andreas, and Wilhelm Ranisch. *Eddica Minora.* Dortmund: Ruhfus, 1903.

Hickes, George. *Linguarum vett. septentrionalium thesaurus grammatico-criticus etarchaeologicus.* Oxford, 1703–1705; rpt. Menston: Scholar, 1970.

Hieatt, Constance B. "Caedmon in Context: Transforming the Formula." *JEGP* 84 (1985): 485–97.

Hoffmann, Otto. *Reimformeln im Westgermanischen.* Diss. Freiberg (Darmstadt), 1885.

Hollander, Lee M., trans. *The Poetic Edda.* Austin: U of Texas P, 1962.

Holtsmark. Anne. "Heroic Poetry and Legendary Sagas." Trans. Peter Foote. *Bibliography of Old Norse-Icelandic Studies* 1965. Copenhagen: Munksgaard, 1966. 9–21.

Hughes, S.F.D. "'Völsunga rímur' and 'Sjúrðar kvæði': Romance and Ballad, Ballad and Dance." *Ballads and Ballad Research.* Ed. Patricia Conroy. Seattle: U of Washington, 1978. 37–45.

Jabbour, Alan Albert. "Memorial Transmission in Old English Poetry." *Chaucer Review* 3 (1969): 174–90.

Jackson, Elizabeth. "Some Contexts and Characteristics of Old Norse Ordering Lists." *SBVS* 23.3 (1991): 111–40.

Jacobson, Pauline, and Geoffrey K. Pullum, eds. *The Nature of Syntactic Representation.* Dordrecht, Holland: Reidel, 1982.

Jesch, Judith. Review of *Dansk Litteratur Historie 1* by Lars Lönnroth, *et al.* in *Saga-Book of the Viking Society* 22.2 (1987): 116–19.

Jones, Alison. "*Daniel* and *Azarias* as Evidence for the Oral-Formulaic Character of Old English Poetry." *Medium Ævum* 35 (1966): 95–102.

Jónsson, Finnur, ed. *Edda Snorra Sturlusonar.* Copenhagen: Gyldendal, 1931.

Jónsson, Guðni. *Eddukvæði.* 2 vols. Reyjavík: Íslendingasagna-útgáfan, 1949.

Kauffmann, Fr. "Das Hildebrandslied." *Philologische Studien: Festgabe für Eduard Sievers.* Halle a. S.: Max Niemeyer, 1896. 124–78.

Keenan, Hugh T. "Children's Literature in Old English." *Children's Literature* 1 (1972): 16–20.

Kellogg, Robert. "A Concordance of Eddic Poetry." Diss. Harvard U, 1958.

———. *A Concordance to Eddic Poetry.* East Lansing, MI: Colleagues, 1988.

———. "Literacy and Orality in the Poetic Edda." In Doane and Pasternack, 89–101.

———. "The Prehistory of Eddic Poetry." In *Poetry*, 187–99.

———. "The South Germanic Oral Tradition." *Franciplegius: Medieval and Linguistic Studies in Honor of Francis Peabody Magoun, Jr.* Eds. Jess B. Bessinger, and Robert P. Creed. New York: New York UP, 1965. 66–74.

Kellogg, Robert, and Robert Scholes. *The Nature of Narrative*. London: Oxford UP, 1966.

Kintgen, Eugene R. "Echoic Repetition in Old English Poetry, Especially *The Dream of the Rood*." *Neuphilologische Mitteilungen* 75 (1974): 202–23.

Kiparsky, Paul. "Oral Poetry: Some Linguistic and Typological Considerations." *Oral Literature and the Formula*. Eds. Benjamin A. Stolz, and Richard S. Shannon, III. Ann Arbor: U of Michigan P, 1976. 73–106.

Kipling, Rudyard. "Recessional." *Complete Verse*. New York: Doubleday, 1989. 327.

Klaeber, F., ed. *Beowulf and the Fight at Finnsburg*. 3rd ed., with supplements. Boston: Heath, 1950.

Klingenberg, Heinz. "*Alvíssmál*: Das Lied vom überweisen Zwerg." *Germanisch-romanische Monatsschrift* 48 (1967): 113–42.

Koskenniemi, Inna. *Repetetive Word Pairs in Old and Early Middle English Prose*. Turku: Turun Yliopisto, 1968.

Krapp, George Philip, and Elliott Van Kirk Dobbie, eds. *The Anglo-Saxon Poetic Records*. 6 vols. New York: Columbia UP, 1932–1953.

Kristjánsson, Jónas. *Eddas and Sagas: Iceland's Medieval Literature*. Trans. Peter Foote. Reykjavík: Hið íslenskabókmenntafélag, 1992.

———. "Stages in the Composition of Eddic Poetry." In *Poetry*, 201–18.

Kuhn, see Neckel.

Kulturhistorisk leksikon for nordisk middelalder. Copenhagen: Rosenkilde og Bagger, 1956–1978.

Lees, Clare A. "Working with Patristic Sources: Language and Context in Old English Homilies." In Frantzen, 157–80.

Lehmann, Winfred P. "The Composition of Eddic Verse." *Studies in Germanic Languages and Literature. In Memory of Fred O. Nolte*. Eds. Erich Hofacker, and Liselotte Dieckmann. St. Louis: Washington UP, 1963. 7–14.

Lerer, Seth. "*Beowulf* and Contemporary Critical Theory." In Bjork and Niles, 325–39.

Liberman, Anatoly. "The Oral-Formulaic Theory and the Style of Old Icelandic Poetry." *The Nordic Languages and Modern Linguistics. 3. Proceedings of the Third International Conference of Nordic and*

General Linguistics. Ed. John Weinstock. Austin: U of Texas P, 1978. 442–53.

Liebermann, Felix, ed. *Die Gesetze der Angelsachsen.* 3 vols. Halle: M. Niemeyer, 1903–1916.

Lindroth, Hjalmar. "Studier över de nordiska dikterna om runornas namn." *Arkiv för nordisk filiologi* 29 (1913): 256–95.

Lindow, John, et. al., eds. *Structure and Meaning in Old Norse Literature.* Odense: Odense UP, 1986.

Littlehales, Henry, ed. *English Fragments from Latin Medieval Service-Books.* EETS es 90. London: Kegan Paul, 1903.

Liuzza, Roy Michael. "On the Dating of *Beowulf.*" *Beowulf: Basic Readings.* Ed. Peter S. Baker. New York: Garland, 1995. 281–97.

Lönnroth, Lars. "The double scene of Arrow-Odd's drinking contest." *Medieval Narrative. A Symposium.* Eds. Hans Bekker Nielsen, *et al.* Odense: Odense UP, 1979. 94–109.

———. *Den dubbla scenen. Muntlig dikting från eddan till Abba.* Stockholm: Prisma, 1978.

———. "Hjalmar's Death Song and the Delivery of Eddic Poetry." *Speculum* 46 (1971): 1–20.

———. "*Iorð fannz æva né upphiminn.* A formula analysis." *Speculum Norroenum. Norse Studies in Meory of Gabriel Turville-Petre.* Eds. Ursula Dronke, *et. al.* Odense: Odense UP, 1981. 310–27.

———. "The New Critics of 1968: Political Persuasion and Literary Scholarship in Scandinavia after the Student Revolution." *Scandinavian Studies* 91 (1981): 30–51.

———. Untitled review of Dronke in *Scandinavica* 9.1 (1970): 53–56.

Lord, Albert Bates. "Homer and Huso II: Narrative Inconsistencies in Homeric and Oral Poetry." *Transactions of the American Philological Association* 69 (1938): 439–45.

———. "Perspectives on Recent Work on Oral Literature." *Oral Literature: Seven Essays.* Ed. Joseph J. Duggan. New York: Barnes, 1975. 1–24.

———. *The Singer of Tales.* Cambridge: Harvard UP, 1960.

———. *The Singer Resumes the Tale.* Ed. Mary Louis Lord. Ithaca: Cornell UP, 1995.

Lynch, Eileen Dorothy. "A Statistical Study of the Collocations in *Beowulf.*" Diss. U of Massachusetts at Amherst, 1972.

Magennis, Hugh. *Images of Community in Old English Poetry.* Cambridge: Cambridge UP, 1996.

Magoun, Francis Peabody, Jr. "Abbreviated Titles for the Poems of the Anglo-Saxon Poetic Corpus." *Etudes anglaises* 8 (1955): 138–46.

———. "The Oral Formulaic Character of Anglo-Saxon Narrative Poetry." *Speculum* 28 (1953): 446–67.

———. "The Theme of the Beasts of Battle in Anglo-Saxon Poetry." *Neuphilologische Mitteilungen* 56 (1955): 81–90.

Malone, Kemp, ed. *Widsith.* London: Methuen, 1936; rev. ed. Copenhagen: Rosenkilde, 1962.

Middle English Dictionary. Ed. Hans Kurath, *et al.* Ann Arbor: U of Michigan P, 1952.

Meletinksy, Eleazar M. "Commonplaces and other elements of folkloric style in Eddic Poetry." In Lindow, 15–31.

Meyer, Richard M. *Die altgermanische Poesie nach ihren formelhaften Elementen beschrieben.* Berlin: Hertz, 1889.

Morris, R., ed. *The Blickling Homilies.* EETS os 58, 63, 73. London: Oxford UP, 1874, 1876, 1880; rpt. 1967.

Morrison, Stephen. "*Beowulf* 698a, 1273a: 'Frofor ond fultum.'" *Notes and Queries* 27 (1980): 193–96.

Neckel, Gustav, ed. *Edda. Die Lieder des Codex Regius nebst verwandten Denkmälern. I. Text.* Heidelberg: Winter, 1914; 4th ed. rev. Hans Kuhn, 1962.

Newton, Sam. *The Origins of Beowulf and the Pre-Viking Kingdom of East Anglia.* Cambridge: Brewer, 1994.

Nicholson, Lewis E. "Oral Techniques in the Composition of Expanded Anglo-Saxon Verses." *PMLA* 78 (1963): 287–92.

Niles, John D. *Beowulf: The Poem and Its Tradition.* Cambridge: Harvard UP, 1983.

Nordal, Sigurður. "Three Essays on *Völuspá.*" Trans. B.S. Benedikz, and J.S. McKinnell. *Saga-Book of the Viking Society* 18 (1970–1973): 79–135.

The Oxford English Dictionary. 2nd ed. Eds. J.A. Simpson, and E.S.C. Weiner. Oxford: Clarendon, 1989.

Ogilvy, J.D.A., and Donald C. Baker. *Reading Beowulf.* Norman, OK: U of Oklahoma P, 1983.

O'Keeffe, Katherine O'Brien. "Diction, Variation, the Formula." In Bjork and Niles, 85–104.

————. *Visible Song: Transitional Literacy in Old English Verse.* Cambridge: Cambridge UP, 1990.

Ólason, Páll Eggert. "Fólgin nöfn í rímum." *Skírnir* 89 (1915): 118–32.

Ólason, Vésteinn. "Frásagnarlist í fornum sögum." *Skírnir* 152 (1978): 166–202.

————. "The Icelandic Ballad as a Medieval Genre." *The European Medieval Ballad. A Symposium.* Ed. Otto Holzapfel. Odense: Odense UP, 1978. 67–74.

Olsen, Alexandra Hennessey. "Oral-Formulaic Research in Old English Studies." *Oral Tradition* 1 (1986): 548–606 (part I) and 3 (1988): 138–90 (part II).

Olsen, Magnus. *Völsunga saga ok Ragnars saga loðbrókar.* Samfund til Udgivelse af gammel nordisk Litteratur. Copenhagen: Möller, 1906–1908.

O'Neil, Wayne A. "Oral-Formulaic Structure in Old English Elegiac Poetry." Diss. U of Wisconsin, 1960.

Ong, Walter. *Orality and Literacy: The Technologizing of the Word.* London: Methuen, 1982.

Opland, Jeff. *Anglo-Saxon Oral Poetry: A Study of the Tradition.* New Haven: Yale UP, 1980.

Orchard, A.P.McD. "Crying wolf: oral style and the *Sermones Lupi.*" *Anglo-Saxon England* 21 (1992): 239–64.

Osborn, Marijane. "*Hleotan* and the Purpose of the Old English *Rune Poem.*" *Folklore* 92.2 (1981): 168–73.

Osborn, Marijane, and Stella Longland. "A Celtic Intruder in the Old English *Rune Poem.*" *Neuphilologische Mitteilungen* 81 (1980): 385–87.

Page, R.I. *"A Most Vile People": Early English Historians on the Vikings.* London: Viking Society, 1987.

Parry, Milman. *The Making of Homeric Verse: the Collected Papers of Milman Parry.* Ed. Adam Parry. Oxford: Oxford UP, 1971.

Poetry in the Scandinavian Middle Ages. The Seventh International Saga Conference. Atti del 12o congresso internazionale di studi sull'alto medioevo. Spoleto 4–10 settembre 1988. Spoleto: Presso la sede del centro studi, 1990.

Propp, Vladimir. *Morphology of the Folktale*. Trans. Laurence Scott. Bloomington: Indiana UP, 1958; rpt. Austin: U of Texas P, 1968.

Quinn, Judy. "The Naming of Eddic Mythological Poems." *Parergon* 8.2 (1990): 97–115.

———. "Verseform and voice in eddic poems: the discourses of *Fáfnismál*." *Arkiv för nordisk filologi* 197 (1992): 100–30.

———. "*Völuspá* and the Composition of Eddic Verse." In *Poetry*, 303–20.

———. "*Völuspá* in Twentieth-Century Scholarship in English." *Old Norse Studies in the New World*. Eds. Geraldine Barnes, Margaret Clunies Ross, and Judy Quinn. Sydney: Dept. of English, U of Sydney, 1994. 120–37.

Quirk, Randolph. "Poetic Language and Old English Metre." *Early English and Norse Studies Presented to Hugh Smith in Honour of His Sixtieth Birthday*. Eds. Arthur Brown, and Peter Foote. London: Methuen, 1963. 150–71.

Richardson, John. "The Critics on the Beach." *Neophilologus* 71 (1987): 114–19.

Riedinger, Anita R. "The Formulaic Relationship Between *Beowulf* and *Andreas*." *Heroic Poetry in the Anglo-Saxon Period: Studies in Honor of Jess B. Bessinger, Jr.* Eds. Helen Damico, and John Leyerle. Studies in Medieval Culture 32. Kalamazoo: Medieval Institute, Western Michigan U, 1993. 283–312.

———. "The Old English Formula in Context." *Speculum* 60.2 (1985): 294–317.

Ritzke-Rutherford, Jean. "Formulaic Microstructure: The Cluster." *The Alliterative Morte Arthure: A Reassesment of the Poem*. Ed. Karl Heinz Göller. Cambridge: Brewer, 1981. 70–82.

Robinson, Fred C. *Beowulf and the Appositive Style*. Knoxville: U of Tennessee P, 1985.

Rogers, H.L. "The Crypto-Psychological Character of the Oral Formula." *English Studies* 67 (1966): 89–102.

Russom, Geoffrey. "Artful Avoidance of the Useful Phrase in *Beowulf, The Battle of Maldon,* and *Fates of the Apostles.*" *Studies in Philology* 75 (1978): 371–90.

———. *"Poculum Mortis* and Germanic Paganism." Plymouth State College, Plymouth, NH. 23 April 1983.

———. Unpublished list of copulative formulas in Old English and Eddic verse.

———. "Verse Translations and the Question of Literacy in *Beowulf." Comparative Research on Oral Traditions: A Memorial for Milman Parry.* Eds. John Miles Foley, and Albert Bates Lord. Columbus: Slavica, 1987. 567–80.

Salomon, Gerhard. *Die Entstehung und Entwickelung der deutschen Zwillingsformeln.* Braunschweig, 1919.

Schmidt, Carl Eduard. *Parallel-Homer oder Index aller homerischen Iterati in lexikalischer Anordnung.* Göttingen: Vandenhoeck, 1885; rpt. 1965.

Selden, Raman, and Peter Widdowson. *A Reader's Guide to Contemporary Literary Theory.* 3rd ed. Lexington: UP of Kentucky, 1993.

Shippey, Thomas A. *Old English Verse.* London: Hutchinson, 1972.

———. *Poems of Wisdom and Learning in Old English.* Cambridge: Brewer, 1976.

———. "Structure and Unity." In Bjork and Niles, 149–74.

Sievers, Eduard, ed. *Heliand.* Halle: Waisenhaus, 1878.

Sigurðsson, Gísli. "On the Classification of Eddic Poetry in View of the Oral Theory." In *Poetry,* 245–55.

Sørensen, Preben Meulengracht. *Saga og samfund.* Copenhagen: Berlingske Forlag, 1977. *Saga and Society.* Trans. John Tucker. Odense: Odense UP, 1993.

Sorrell, Paul. "Oaks, ships, riddles and the Old English *Rune Poem." Anglo-Saxon England* 19 (1990): 103–16.

Stanley, E.G. "Notes on the Text of *Christ and Satan:* And on *The Riming Poem* and *The Rune Poem,* Chiefly on Wynn, Wen and Wenne." *Notes and Queries.* 229.4 (Dec., 1984): 443–53.

Steblin-Kamenskij, M.I. "Some Considerations on Approaches to Medieval Literature." *Mediaeval Scandinavia* 8 (1975): 187–91.

Stephens, John. "The Poet and *Atlakviða*. Variations on some themes." *Iceland and the Mediaeval World*. Eds. Gabriel Turville-Petre, and John Stanley Martin. Clayton, Australia: Wilke, 1974. 52–62.

Stevenson, William H., ed. *Asser's Life of King Alfred*. Oxford: Clarendon, 1904; rpt. 1959.

Sveinsson, Einar Ól. *Íslenzkar bókmenntir í fornöld*. Reykjavík: Almenna bókafélagið, 1962.

Taylor, Paul Beekman. "Old Norse Heroic Poetry. A Study of Tradition in the Heroic Poems of the *Poetic Edda*." Diss. Brown U, 1961.

———. "The Structure of the *Völundarkviða*." *Neophilologus* 47 (1963): 228–36.

Tolkien, Christopher, trans. & ed. *The Saga of King Heidrek the Wise*. London: Nelson, 1960.

Toller, see Bosworth.

Turville-Petre, E.O.G. *Origins of Icelandic Literature*. Oxford: Clarendon, 1953.

Venezky, Richard L., and Antonette diPaolo Healey, compilers. *A Microfiche Concordance to Old English*. Published by the Dictionary of Old English Project, Centre for Medieval Studies, U of Toronto. Toronto: U of Toronto P, 1980.

Vihman, Marilyn May. "Formulas in First and Second Language Acquisition." *Exceptional Language and Linguistics*. Eds. Loraine K. Obler and Lise Menn. New York: Academic, 1982. 261–84.

Watkins, Calvert. "Language of Gods and Language of Men: Remarks on Some Indo-European Metalinguistic Traditions." *Myth and Law among the Indo-Europeans: Studies in Indo-European Comparative Mythology*. Ed. Jaan Puhvel. Berkeley: U of California P, 1970. 1–17.

Watts, Ann Chalmers. *The Lyre and the Harp*. New Haven: Yale UP, 1969.

Whallon, William. "The Diction of *Beowulf*." *PMLA* 76 (1961): 309–19.

———. *Formula, Character and Context: Studies in Homeric, Old English and Old Testament Poetry*. Cambridge: Harvard UP, 1969.

Whitelock, Dorothy. *The Audience of Beowulf*. Oxford: Clarendon, 1951.

———. "Wulfstan at York." *Franciplegius: Medieval and Linguistic Studies in Honor of Francis Peabody Magoun, Jr*. Eds. Jess B.

Bessinger, Jr., and Robert P. Creed. New York: New York UP, 1965. 214–31.

Whitman, F.H. "The Meaning of 'Formulaic' in Old English Verse Composition." *Neuphilologische Mitteilungen* 76 (1975): 529–37.

Williams, Blanche Colton. *Gnomic Poetry in Anglo-Saxon.* New York: Columbia UP, 1914.

Index